Reading Modernity, Modernism and Religion Today

Feelings of rootlessness, fragmentation and loneliness are endemic in today's secular societies. In the late nineteenth century, Émile Durkheim described this kind of social malaise as anomie, a concept this book locates within a historical narrative of the emergence of Modernism from Modernity. The book focuses on two representative figures, Benedictus de Spinoza and Vincent van Gogh, on whose works it offers significant new perspectives. Spinoza drew up a blueprint for Modernity, which is to say, the cultural transformations that took place as a result of the Scientific Revolution and the Protestant Reformation. In counterpoint to his overriding confidence in reason, a persistent current in Spinoza's writing shows how concerned he was about a possible loss of confidence in his governing idea of a single Substance, the philosophical God, with which he sought to replace the creator God of the Bible. In promoting art as a means of filling the gap left by the absence of Spinoza's philosophical God and the failures of traditional Christianity, Van Gogh also discovered the limitations of the vocation to which he had dedicated himself. He concluded that in the tension between art and anomie, a new kind of religious sensibility and understanding might emerge. This remains the case in the current postmodern cultural phase when fragmentation and incoherence are summoning up new assessments and re-configurations of values promoting new forms of solidarity, dialogue and religious understanding.

Patrick Grant is Professor Emeritus at the University of Victoria, British Columbia, Canada. He has published widely on relationships amongst literature, religion and secularism. He has a special interest in literature of the English Renaissance, literary theory, and the literature and culture of modern Northern Ireland. He has published a series of books on the letters of Vincent van Gogh.

Routledge Focus on Literature

Dreams in Chinese Fiction
Spiritism, Aestheticism, and Nationalism
Johannes D. Kaminski

Remapping Energopolitics
Blue Humanities, Geophilosophy and Sri Lankan Minor Writings
Abhisek Ghosal

Colonial Philippines in Italian Travel Writing
"Italians" Interpreting Difference
Jillian Loise Melchor

Essays on The Glass Menagerie
Truth in the Pleasant Disguise of Illusion
Tania Chakravertty

Margaret Wise Brown's Experimental Art
The Modernist Picture Book
Julia Pond

Tolkien and the Kalevala
Jyrki Korpua

Elevating Humanity via Africana Womanism
Clenora Hudson (Weems)

Reading Modernity, Modernism and Religion Today
Spinoza and Van Gogh
Patrick Grant

For more information about this series, please visit: www.routledge.com/Routledge-Focus-on-Literature/book-series/RFLT

Reading Modernity, Modernism and Religion Today

Spinoza and Van Gogh

Patrick Grant

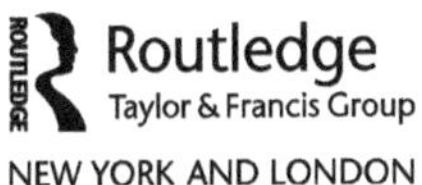

NEW YORK AND LONDON

First published 2025
by Routledge
605 Third Avenue, New York, NY 10158

and by Routledge
4 Park Square, Milton Park, Abingdon, Oxon, OX14 4RN

Routledge is an imprint of the Taylor & Francis Group, an informa business

ISBN: 9781032896694 (hbk)
ISBN: 9781032902722 (pbk)
ISBN: 9781003546856 (ebk)

DOI: 10.4324/9781003546856

Typeset in Times New Roman
by KnowledgeWorks Global Ltd.

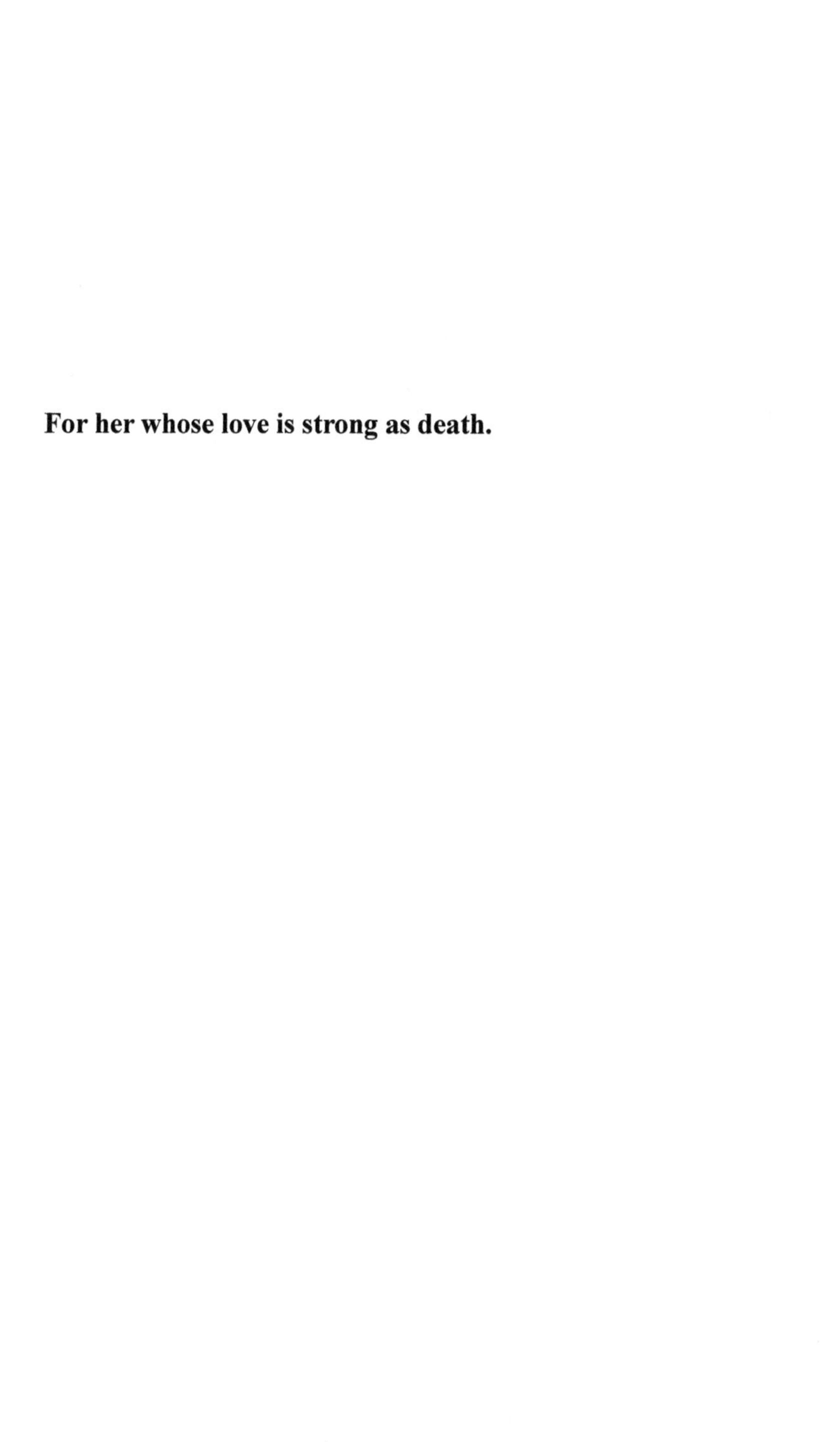

For her whose love is strong as death.

Contents

Preface

Feelings of rootlessness, fragmentation and loneliness are endemic in today's secular societies. In the late nineteenth century, Émile Durkheim described this kind of social malaise as *anomie*, a concept which, in the following chapters, I locate within a historical narrative of the emergence of Modernism from Modernity. In so doing, I focus on two representative figures, Benedictus de Spinoza and Vincent van Gogh, on whose works I also attempt to offer some new perspectives, with a view to assessing how their critique of religion pertains to discussions of that topic today.

Spinoza drew up a blueprint for Modernity, which is to say the cultural transformations that took place as a result of the Scientific Revolution and the Protestant Reformation. In counterpoint to his overriding confidence in reason, a persistent undercurrent in Spinoza's writing shows how concerned he was about a possible loss of confidence in his governing idea of a single Substance, the philosophical God, with which he sought to replace the creator God of the Bible. Through a series of developments in the following centuries, Spinoza's apprehensions were in fact realized, resulting in the condition described by Durkheim as *anomie*.

In his personal life, Van Gogh wrestled constantly with *anomie*, which he saw also as a sign of the times. As a representative of the Modernist movement that responded to the cultural crises of the end of the nineteenth century that gave rise to *anomie*, Van Gogh's career recapitulated the historical narrative of the emergence of Modernism from Modernity, a fact that deepens and intensifies his significance today. In promoting art as a means of filling the gap left by the absence of Spinoza's philosophical God and the failures of traditional Christianity, Van Gogh also discovered the limitations of the vocation to which he had dedicated himself. He concluded that in the tension between art and *anomie*, a new kind of religious sensibility and understanding might emerge. This remains the case in the current cultural phase when fragmentation and incoherence are summoning up new assessments and reconfigurations of values promoting new forms of solidarity, dialogue and religious understanding.

In his monumental study, *Religion in Human Evolution* (Cambridge, MA: Harvard University Press, 2011), Robert N. Bellah imagines that "there will be readers who will like the cases and throw away the argument", then adding, "that is fine with me" (p. xvii). As far as the present book is concerned, I imagine that there will be readers who, likewise, will be more interested in the two main cases than in the cultural narrative within which I place them. As with Bellah, this is fine with me, if only because no single, containing argument or theory accounts sufficiently for the complexity of the phenomena to be explained, and any single cultural narrative that pre-empts alternative ways of reading is incapable of carrying forward the kinds of exchange on which any vital cultural tradition depends.

Nonetheless, effective discussions also need to be conducted from an identifiable point of view, which, in turn, is inseparable from the networks of historical transmission and relationship enabling that point of view to be formulated and expressed in the first place. If nothing is affirmed, criticism is pointless – indeed, there would be no criticism at all – and no enhanced understanding could take place. And so, in the present study, my main affirmations about *anomie* and religion are anchored in the case studies, which in turn represent something of the historical and cultural conditions from which the affirmations emerge. In so far as the cases observe appropriate scholarly standards and are convincing, they can be read independently, perhaps with benefit. Yet, without the containing narrative, the scholarly studies risk being sidelined as specialised and academic, just as, without the detailed arguments, the cultural narrative is likely to remain speculative and superficial. In the tension between these poles, new perspectives and understandings can be negotiated and discovered. In turn, maintaining and negotiating this tension is itself a method of enquiry that can profitably be adopted in further studies aiming to ameliorate the kinds of incoherence that this book undertakes to describe.

1 Introduction

The language mosaic

We cannot stand outside ourselves sufficiently to survey the whole of which we are a part, but neither is our knowledge of the world entirely unreliable.[1] We trawl, as it were, with the nets we are given, and what we catch is real, even though a great deal slips through the mesh.[2] How we interpret what we manage to catch often gives rise to disagreements, but not every interpretation of those disagreements is equally valid. If this was not the case, no meaningful change could occur, and whatever power structures happened to be in place could not effectively be challenged because there would be no way to prefer one set of arguments about them to another. The apparent freedoms afforded by a thoroughgoing relativism would turn out, after all, to be depressingly conservative.

By raising the question of interpretation I have, however indirectly, introduced the fact that *Homo sapiens* is distinguished especially by language. The rapid symbolic speech that emerged some 200,000 years ago enabled human civilization to develop in a comparatively short period of time. It also enabled us to acquire control over nature to the degree that our existence now stands under threat from the very forces we have managed to unleash; nuclear weapons and climate change would, to adapt the well-known words of Robert Frost, "suffice" to put an end to us.[3] Despite the conscionable voices that have been sounding the alarm for decades, we have so far talked ourselves out of doing enough about it, and arguing, as some people do, as if climate science is no more or less valid than other interpretations, is to encourage a disaster that would be a highly convincing refutation of the strong form of relativism, if anyone were around to make the point.

Although the origins of human language remain obscure, the role of language in promoting the ascendency of *Homo sapiens* is not. As Merlin Donald argues,[4] our rapid symbolic speech supplemented cognitive abilities that had already evolved. Donald points to the fact that deaf-mute children can perform tasks and participate in games and other social interactions that are beyond the capacity of chimpanzees, the primates which resemble us most closely (21).

DOI: 10.4324/9781003546856-1

Differences in cognitive ability are therefore not dependent on spoken language, which has, nonetheless, vastly enhanced our cognitive range. Today, the process of enhancement continues, especially by way of information technology, and is effecting changes perhaps more profound and further-reaching than Gutenberg. At present, we cannot adequately assess the full immensity of these changes, though a great deal of helpful work has been done on the topic.[5]

As Donald argues, language depends on the evolutionary gains that set up the conditions for language to emerge (233). He reminds us of Darwin's observation that human speech is rooted in the cries and signals we share with other animals – a "rudimentary song" (34) expressing alarm, pain, joy, triumph and so on. A cry of alarm is embodied and is a participatory experience rather than a considered assessment of a state of affairs objectively set over against us. The same holds for gestures – a topic Darwin does not explore – which also communicate embodied meanings in which we participate even as we consider them objectively. Since Kant, it is commonplace to acknowledge that perception actively shapes the world and does not just passively record it, even though we need to stop short of claiming that perception actually constitutes the things we observe. As Robert N. Bellah writes, "we are one part of the world knowing selectively other parts of the world. Our knowledge is reliable enough, given all the possibilities of fallibility, but it is partial, it is context-dependent".[6]

Here, it is also worth emphasizing that human language and communication systems are not a single, unified set, but a mosaic of structures and skills that are more or less successfully synthesized. A spontaneous cry of alarm is auditory and a gesture of defiance is visual, but we can imagine how these might merge to convey a single message – for instance, "You are frightening me; back off!" The fact that the centre in the brain that processes sound and the centre that processes verbal information are different[7] does not prevent the message from appearing as the utterance of a unified subject. In an analogous way, the music of a poem and its conceptual sense can co-exist in a single experience, as the separate physiological bases of the rhythmic and conceptual elements are taken up into a satisfying and convincing synthesis.

Over time, additional skills were added to the basic repertoire of cries and gestures, with spoken language eventually occupying a pre-eminent position. But spoken language did not dispense with the cries and the gestures which we continue to use, and which still permeate our day-to-day communication. As Donald shows, bodily gestures developed towards mimetic displays, and, through spoken language, into ritual, dance and storytelling.[8] Through stories, people found a way to represent their connections to nature, the cosmos and to one another within a social group. Our earliest stories, or myths, therefore record the coming to consciousness of fundamental questions about human existence, and something of the archetypal power of the oral traditions within which mythic thinking took shape remains in the ancient epics that were recorded with the advent of writing, such as the *Iliad* and the *Odyssey*, the oldest strata of the Bible, and the *Mahabharata*.[9] In these texts, myth is taken up into extended narratives that describe the formation of cultural identity over time. The eventual development of second-order thinking (reflection on the process itself of thinking) was powerfully re-enforced by the advent of writing, which rapidly expanded the opportunity for reflective criticism (a written text could be interrogated at leisure). The conceptual and analytical tools that were developed during the period loosely described as the Axial Age (c. 900–200 BCE) brought about far-reaching changes in the structure and organization of human society,[10] and during this process, logic and conceptual coherence frequently came into conflict with the metaphoric and symbolic languages that were fundamental to mythological thinking. The explanations offered by these different (if overlapping) capabilities of language are often uneasily synthesized, as we see today not least in the widespread confrontations between scientific empiricism and traditional religious beliefs and practices. Amongst other things, such confrontations remind us that human communication is a mosaic in which different elements jostle, often combining but often at odds, surprisingly fallible and yet with powerful transformative capabilities.

Dialogue, anomie and the conservation of gains

In the process of evolution, the conservation of gains ensures that new skills incorporate earlier ones, so that, in a way, we remain all that we have been. Consequently, although conceptual thinking affords many advantages, we are still motivated by the stories and symbols that shape our emotions and desires. Jonathan Swift's reminder that we are *rationis capax* (capable of reason) is a prudent corrective to the Aristotelian definition that a human being is *animal rationale* (a rational animal). Swift is right: reason does not fully control our emotions and other impulses which are often more adequately engaged and managed by communication skills emergent at earlier, key stages of our development. Underestimating the continuing influence of these skills on our everyday behaviour causes distortions that can destabilize the whole, complex edifice. For this reason, I have argued elsewhere for the need to cultivate dialogue in as many spheres of discourse as possible. Dialogue, that is, engages the entire spectrum of our evolved communication skills, beginning with an immediate, pre-linguistic recognition that the other whom we meet face to face has a sentience and intentionality akin to my own while also being different and not wholly accessible.[11] The phenomenology of this profoundly human, primary communication is compellingly explored by Emmanuel Levinas,[12] and I want to claim that, in Levinas' sense, the primordial, personal presence of the other remains fundamental to dialogue, which then also incorporates mimesis (or gesture) and narrative, as well as concepts and logical thinking. As Gadamer points out, through dialogue the horizons of the interlocutors merge to make something new from the differences that inform their encounter. The outcome is therefore more than an exchange of opinions or ideas. Rather, it is an enhanced way of thinking and seeing that reaches into the recesses of the body, including its feeling-structures and pre-articulate habits and prejudices, to forge a different disposition, a change of attitude in the whole person, as well as new ideas.[13] In this sense, dialogue resembles art, a fact that art itself invites us to discover and share.

As is the case with dialogue, through language in general we are connected to the world and also placed over and against it, moved by a desire to unite with the other in understanding, to have the word become flesh even though we only ever manage to do this imperfectly.[14] The fault lines run not only between ourselves and the world but also within language itself, which, as we see, is riven by gaps and fissures as different communication skills, fit for different purposes, are sometimes complementary but often not. For instance, the scientific theory of evolution and the opening chapters of Genesis offer contradictory explanations of how our world came to be. In a different sphere of discourse, Christopher Marlowe's powerfully rhythmic "mighty line" (the newly discovered dramatic use of iambic pentameter) expresses the triumphant self-will that blinds Dr. Faustus to how flawed his thinking actually is. Here, the tension between what is conveyed by the music of the language and by its conceptual content produces an arresting portrait of a gifted but hubristic overreacher who is impressive but also self-deluded. The contesting elements within the language therefore work in the service of Marlowe's art, whereas, in the first example, the explanatory power of myth and scientific theory remain at odds and can be reconciled only if we see them as different kinds of discourse, offering different kinds of explanation.

As a result of this state of affairs, in accounting for what we are we tell the best stories and offer the best explanations we can. To be convincing, these stories and explanations need continually to be tested against experience and compared to each other. The outcomes, though less than completely satisfying, are at best, as I began by saying, not unreliable, and yet, today, and for roughly the past half century, the prevailing cultural trend loosely described as postmodernism[15] has expressed a plentifully abundant impatience with notions such as stable meaning, containing narratives, dependable foundations, explanations and the like. In his influential book, *The Postmodern Condition. A Report on Knowledge*, Jean-François Lyotard states, in an often-cited sentence: "Simplifying to the extreme, I define postmodern as incredulity towards metanarratives".[16] Lyotard points here to a common element in a wide range of postmodern discourses, namely, the undermining not only of commonly accepted values, but also of the narratives that afford them authority. The claims of traditional religion, Enlightenment reason and Romantic organic unity are subjected to an irreverently ingenious, solvent scepticism, as God, Reason and Nature are interrogated by a hermeneutic of suspicion and discovered to be emperors without clothes. And yet, a consequent, widespread sense of disenchantment is not to be laid at the feet of postmodernism alone. Already in the late nineteenth century, the cultural crisis that gave rise to the

Modernist movement was all too well aware of a widespread loss of faith in these same traditional lodestars. The difference is that, in contrast to postmodernism, the High Modernists struggled to recover something of what had been lost, rescued from the cultural detritus. Value in itself was, as it were, the last man standing when postmodernism took the field, leading an offensive that has had mixed results. On the one hand, the typical postmodernist deployment of mobile units of playfully ironic arguments that are subversive of hierarchy, authoritarian cant and traditional certainties has blown like a gale of bracing air, dispelling all manner of hypocrisy and pretension. On the other hand, the gains have come at a price, and, like the late capitalism that it reproduces and celebrates, postmodernism is trapped in a process of perpetual circulation without purpose or meaning other than yet more production, consumption and libidinal play.

Already in 1979, Lyotard had described a further aspect of postmodernism that has, in the twenty-first century, become all-too obvious; that is, nowadays information technology and the digital revolution have made unimaginably vast amounts of information instantaneously and universally available, and in so doing have brought far-reaching and incalculable benefits. Yet, one further, also far-reaching, result is that an unmanageable surplus of information all too readily overwhelms and short-circuits coherent understanding. We are more and more on the move, as it were, in the attempt just to keep up, and the upshot is that serious enquiries about foundations are too frequently replaced by performative ingenuities and the force of individual will. In addition, the fragmenting impact of the tsunamis of information, misinformation and disinformation available through digital communication has done much to erode public discourse, trust in public institutions and respect for expertise. One result is an ever more rapidly diffused and widespread sense of rootlessness and insecurity, of dislocation from sustaining meaning, narrative coherence and solidarity.

In 2023, the Surgeon General of the United States published an 81-page advisory[17] on "Our Epidemic of Loneliness and Isolation", in which he expresses concern about this kind of rootlessness, and how an alarmingly increasing number of people in the United States report feeling "isolated, invisible, and insignificant" (4). This widespread sense of isolation has led, in turn, to an erosion of "trust in each other and major institutions", and to a "fraying of the social fabric" (13). The Surgeon General goes on to point out that although recent advances in communications technology have brought benefits, there are also liabilities: "several examples of harms include technology that displaces in-person engagement, monopolizes our attention, reduces the quality of our interactions, and even our self-esteem" (20). Suicide rates have soared and are, especially amongst men who live alone, strongly associated with loneliness. In addition, as inter-personal and social networks weaken, "society becomes more polarized" (44) and "growing ideological divisions in the U.S. are fueling scepticism and even animosity between groups" (44), leading, in turn, to a greatly exacerbated "identity-based extremism and violence" (44). The Surgeon General worries that a further result of chronic loneliness is that "we will continue to splinter and divide until we can no longer stand as a community or a country" (4). He does not explain how loneliness plays a role in fomenting the ideological clashes that are producing the animosity and violence about which he worries. However, already in 1951, Hannah Arendt had provided an explanation of this phenomenon by arguing that loneliness is a necessary forerunner of totalitarianism. That is, totalitarian regimes exploit loneliness in order to impose their own ideological propaganda. This strategy is effective because when loneliness is sufficiently debilitating, it causes people to feel uprooted – "isolated, invisible, and insignificant," as the Surgeon General explains. In this condition, people's self-esteem is diminished and they become sceptical, lacking in trust, and totalitarian regimes then moves in to supply a new sense of identity and belonging. Yet, paradoxically, in order to succeed, totalitarianism needs to preserve people's isolation. That is, totalitarian ideology permits no deviation and takes steps to suppress independent thinking. In so doing, it obliterates the space between people within which critical argument and dialogue can take place, and the most radical means of this suppression is violence, whether against dissident insiders or outsiders who resist the totalizing logic of the all-containing system. Hannah Arendt concludes that terror is a hallmark of totalitarian regimes, and it is the main instrument for ensuring their survival.[18]

The Surgeon General's epidemic of loneliness therefore has more ominous implications than his report acknowledges. Broadly, in Western secular societies, and especially the United States – "the cruellest form of capitalism in the world" according to the far-from radical, former presidential adviser, Robert Reich[19] – peoples' self-interest, endless competitiveness and exaggerated individualism consign them to a lonely crowd restlessly in search of gratification within an infinitely expanding market that is without sustaining meaning or purpose beyond reproducing itself. It is not surprising that isolation and loneliness, combined with a loss of shared meaning and value, make the lonely crowd of uprooted, atomized individuals vulnerable to whatever light-sleeping authoritarianism is waiting in the wings. Ironically, the postmodern hermeneutic of suspicion has managed to undermine traditional certainties to the point where the appeal of authoritarianism, with its promise of belonging, meaning and identity, has become much more difficult to resist. Seen in this light, and despite its rejection of metanarratives, postmodernism itself appears as part of a larger, complexly layered story.

In the late nineteenth century, Émile Durkheim (1858–1917) had already understood how a dominant mass-commodity culture driven by hyper-industrialization and *laissez-faire* capitalism had brought about a loosening of traditional bonds and an increase in isolation, rootlessness and loneliness. He saw these problems as exacerbated by a new kind of free-floating desire ("malady of the infinite") ungoverned by traditional norms and unable to find satisfaction in commodity consumption alone. Durkheim called this condition *anomie*, or "normlessness", and he argued that it led to destructive behaviour, including suicide.[20]

Today, Durkheim's ideas about *anomie* continue to be of interest in sociology, criminology and studies on the automation of industry, amongst others.[21] Here, I am placing the term in a broader context as a precursor of the current postmodern cultural phase in which "normlessness" is often welcomed as liberating, and the "malady of the infinite" is celebrated as a joyous release from oppressive constraints. Yet, as the Surgeon General and Hannah Arendt insist, along Durkheim's lines, an aggregate of lonely individuals does not produce a viable human community; a cacophony of monologues does not produce dialogue; a dismissal of narrative does not support the search for meaning and identity. In short, the absence of norms and values does not leave people feeling liberated; it makes them feel isolated and vulnerable to whatever authoritarian agencies are prepared to declare is necessary to make up for what is missing.

So far, I have described postmodernism as a style or set of attitudes, and I have pointed to trends that are easy to recognize because of their prevalence in the early twenty-first century *zeitgeist* they have helped to shape. But, following Lyotard, I am aware also of "simplifying in the extreme", and to redress the balance it is worth pointing out that in a pluralist, secular society, a great many cultural traditions co-exist and are sustained by values often antithetical to a merely libidinal consumerism within the free play of the market. These many traditions jostle and, as Charles Taylor says, "fragilize" each other,[22] in which case, pluralism ironically turns out to be also an example of dividing to conquer. As Walter Benjamin argues, capitalism was originally a parasitic growth on Christianity but it has now become the host, and the bourgeois churches have by and large re-shaped themselves in its image. Mirroring this state of affairs, the competitive religious pluralism in today's secular societies effectively divides each religious group from the other, thereby ensuring that none of them poses a threat to the regular order of business. Whatever authority we might accord to Benjamin's assertion that capitalism is a religion,[23] its dominance in Western secular states throws into relief how difficult it is for the vast mosaic of beliefs, narratives and practices available today to converge in the interests of any agreed-upon and consciously sought-after, humanizing solidarity that might bring us beyond the instrumentalism, exaggerated individualism and impersonal mechanisms of a free-market system that inevitably casts people into isolation, a sense of uprootedness and a pervasive *anomie*. As things stand, in today's religion supermarket,[24] the established, main religious traditions – together with their innumerable internal offshoots and factions – find themselves displayed on an equal footing with new-age cults, crackpot pseudo-mysticism, and the like, together with the rich array of Eastern practices and wisdom traditions to which the West, in the past century or so, has had unprecedented access. How so many contending voices might converge towards common goals affirming the dignity of persons, universal human rights and the common good is not easy to see. Piecemeal, is one answer, and it is not negligible, however insufficient. Nonetheless, although the lineaments of a new manner or style of understanding of religion remain inchoate, they are detectable in and through many networks of people and agencies across every tradition bent on seeking a new spirit of exchange and communion beyond self-interest and with the power to transfigure interpersonal relationships and the social fabric together.[25] A broadly religious, or post-religious, sensibility – something as yet with "no name", as Vincent van Gogh writes – would not be a new beginning that enables us, somehow, to move forward without the benefits accruing from the earlier, formative phases of the story. Rather, it would recapitulate and transfigure those earlier gains, so that their relevance becomes evident in new ways. As I have suggested, this is also the case with the evolution of human language and culture, and based on the same idea of recapitulation, I want to place postmodernism in the context of Modernism (arising from a cultural crisis in the late nineteenth century) and of Modernity (arising from a cultural crisis in the sixteenth and seventeenth centuries). The evolution that this historical narrative helps us to see can, in turn, provide bearings for assessing the challenges posed by *anomie* today. With these points in mind, I take Benedictus de Spinoza and Vincent van Gogh to epitomize the central concerns of the two crucial periods under consideration. Religion was a central concern for both of them, but not just as a matter of doctrines and propositions. Rather, their views on religion were part of the tangled skein of their personal embeddedness in the larger cultural movements that they represent. The transvaluations of value in which they participated entail a whole new way of viewing the world, rather than just the introduction of new ideas or theories presented as options from which to choose. New values take hold of the whole person. They reach down through the layers of ourselves into the recesses of the body that determine our most primitive encounters with others, in turn engaging the different emotional and rational needs expressed through the entire range of our communication skills. By attending in detail to Spinoza and Van Gogh, we can make contact with these kinds of complexity, through which, in turn, we can better understand the transformative power of their work within the culture at large, including their pertinence to the status and possibilities of religion today.

Spinoza and Van Gogh: narratives of transformation

In the following pages, I want to suggest that Spinoza, who, with astonishing prescience anticipated the development of modern secularism, was also a prophet of *anomie*. That is, throughout his work, a disturbing undercurrent registers his unease about the prospect of the radical disorientations that would follow if his metaphysical first principles failed to hold at the centre, which in fact, over time, turned out to be the case. At the end of the nineteenth century, Durkheim's *anomie* describes a malaise of the very kind that had caused Spinoza's concern. In turn, throughout his life, Vincent van Gogh struggled continuously with *anomie*, and part of his remarkable appeal today arises from the fact that his life and work recapitulate the story itself of the emergence of Modernism from Modernity; however, much of this aspect of his work has remained unnoticed.[26] As a painter, Van Gogh presented the aesthetic as a main bulwark against *anomie*, and yet, towards the end of his life, he realized that the aesthetic did not suffice, and he gestured, however uncertainly, towards a new kind of spiritual understanding that would bridge the gap between art and life. The open question that he posed remains with us, as the intimations of some broadly diffused spiritual aspiration to which he pointed can be felt today as a surplus, inchoate but in excess of a prevailing secular scepticism. A not-yet named transvaluation of what religion might mean is, as Van Gogh thought, in process, and he felt that its development was exigent because he experienced its absence (almost) so strongly.

At the present time, the secular, neo-liberal West would do well to reconsider the strengths of its own cultural history, if only because, without a sufficient sense of identity informed by sustaining narratives and values, no real meeting with others can take place. As Hans Georg Gadamer points out, through dialogue, different pre-judgements, narratives and values are modified in the production of some further, enhanced understanding. By contrast, *anomie*, which has been re-enforced and deepened in the current postmodern cultural phase, has left us busily sawing at the branch on which we are sitting.

This is not to say that the Western cultural heritage is without contradictions and discontinuities beyond the scope of any single overview, and Lyotard is right to warn us against thinking otherwise. And yet, values, identities and narratives can be beneficially shared even if they are imperfectly formulated and incompletely described. For example, Spinoza's writings do not stand alone but can be situated within a network of further narratives that draw us back eventually to the ancient Mediterranean civilizations which underpin the main cultural traditions of Western Europe. In turn, we might then look further back to the agricultural revolution of some 12,000 years ago which produced the food surpluses that provided thinkers and scholars with leisure to explore the possibility of transcending traditional narratives about tribal or group identity and to explore the idea of promoting universal values within a new kind of civilized order. In the ancient Greek philosophers, the later prophetic books of the Hebrew scriptures, Confucianism, the Upanishads, the Buddhist sutras and, later, in Christianity and Islam, a recurring claim is that liberation is achieved by adherence to a transcendent principle or reality, regardless of kin, class, tribal allegiance, social status and traditional cult practice. The period of this monumental development in human thought was named the Axial Age by Karl Jaspers, and it profoundly affected the organization of human society, as well as what it means to be a person.[27] A further main point of emphasis amongst Axial Age thinkers was that the curtailment of ego gratification was necessary if we are to live according to values to which humanity as a whole should aspire. Yet, Axial Age thinking also developed closed systems of thought and belief, supported by a highly developed conceptual apparatus and promulgated through dogma. Confrontations between the systematic, conceptually framed teachings of the Axial Age religions and older mythological and symbolic ways of thinking veered between outright rejection of the ancient myths and an appropriation of them by way of allegory, claiming that the myths were veiled anticipations of truths later revealed. These appropriations were never comfortable and have remained problematic down to and including the present.

These retrospective remarks are relevant to what I want to say about Spinoza because Modernity, heralded by the Scientific Revolution and the Protestant Reformation, stood so radically opposed to the Axial Age metaphysical foundations of Medieval Christianity[28] and can be adequately understood only in relation to that rejection which, as is so often the case, was less than a complete repudiation. At present, in our democratic, secular societies, in contrast to the Middle Ages, no closed system of religious belief prevails, and thoughtful adherents of the traditional Axial Age religions no longer insist on exclusive access to the saving truth. Yet, traditional Axial Age teachings about the curtailing of self-centred acquisitiveness and promoting universal values and the equality of persons remain far from irrelevant. The fact that these ideals are often espoused today by non-believers indicates the degree to which morality has become a touchstone for religion rather than the reverse, as in past times. Still, the complex historical narrative that enabled such freedoms, moral principles and critical perspectives to develop cannot be discarded without to some degree jeopardizing those same freedoms. Again, as with evolution, including the evolution of language, attempts to dispense with gains made at earlier stages of development cause distortions that make the whole edifice vulnerable. As Charles Taylor writes, there is "no place for unproblematic breaks with a past which is simply left behind us",[29] and one function of traditional religion today is to recapitulate, to re-enact, the story of the past as an *anamnesis*, a making present of values that continue to assist and sustain. The emotional exigencies of our earliest utterances, the repertoire of gestures, the metaphorical interconnectedness between ourselves and the world expressed in myth, the sense of personal and group identity shaped by narrative, together with understandings that are conceptually formulated continue to influence how we view and experience the world. An authentic religious *anamnesis* holds these elements together, as it opens also on the encompassing mystery of the origins and meaning of life. All this is quite different from today's standard identification of religion with doctrine and denominational allegiance.

With the advent of Modernism at the end of the nineteenth century, and as Van Gogh makes clear, art did much to supply what was missing with the decline of traditional Christian observance in the secularized West. Today, major art exhibitions resemble secular pilgrimage sites, as a vast tourist industry thrives on the artistic wealth of Europe's past (a great deal of it religious), visited, for the most part, for its aesthetic appeal rather than for religious or moral reasons.[30] And yet, a main difference between art and religion is that religion requires shared commitments, practices and beliefs pertaining to the ultimate conditions of existence, while also prescribing rules for how to live and how to treat and relate to others.[31] Art does not do this and the gap between art and more fully communal ways of living and understanding, such as religion might enable, was, for Van Gogh, (as we shall see) a major challenge of a kind that remains very much alive. On the moral front, the fact that organized religion has often failed to act humanely is all-too clear as a matter of historical record, and the denunciation of crimes committed in the name of religion should, at the very least, clarify what religion should not be. In short, the secular critique, such as Spinoza spearheaded, helps to reveal the meaning and value of religion to the religions themselves, and if no value survives that critique, religion has no future, as many of its secular critics have already decided. Yet, religion also addresses perennial human needs and aspirations which are best not ignored, if only because those needs and aspirations then became vulnerable to the kinds of authoritarian propaganda that appear to provide an answer, as Hannah Arendt has pointed out.

I began by saying that no account of what we are tells the whole story because we cannot occupy a neutral position in order to observe the whole of which we are a part. Rather, we tell the best stories we can, and in so doing, as I have also suggested, it is easy to underestimate the continuing influence of the cultural achievements that allow those stories to be told as we are now able to tell them. In the West, the long battle for freedom of conscience, religion, expression and enquiry was fought over centuries, its history interwoven with commensurate achievements in art, science and philosophy that promote, amongst other things, a high evaluation of the dignity of persons and of universal human rights. That we are free within limits because we stand on the shoulders of these giant accomplishments is clear on a little reflection. And yet, today, the sheer complexity of what we can survey because of the technological gains that are part of that same history is all but overwhelming. In turn, this complexity has done much to promote the postmodern zeitgeist marked by scepticism, relativism and loss of faith in the narratives that, ironically, have shaped the postmodern zeitgeist itself. Not surprisingly, the undermining of foundations together with a prevailing scepticism about containing narratives have produced the widespread feelings of rootlessness that the Surgeon General describes. An effective antidote would not be yet another narrative requiring universal assent, but, rather, broad networks of enquiry and explanation conducted by people who are aware of the state of the question and of their own insertion into a complex, living tradition. Dialogical encounters, either within a culture or between cultures, need not surrender the identity and integrity of the participants, even as each stands open to new consolidations and unexpected syntheses emergent from a fusing of different horizons. Exchanges at a superficial level, in the interests of expediency or entertainment or the avoidance of patient effort, will not achieve much because they do not reach sufficiently into the bodily rootedness of our enculturated habits of thought, the feeling-structures in which commitment is embedded and where real change can occur. Taking pleasure in a free play of surfaces and the fast and fashionable cycle of production and consumption has its gratifications, but that kind of perpetual serendipity produces nothing of value, rather as an unanchored thread endlessly, dexterously on the move is incapable of making a stable pattern or stitching anything together. By contrast, networks of encounter and exchange in which considered points of view are brought to bear can effectively explore common goals in a spirit that preserves diversity while seeking consensus. Local cultures and ancient traditions can then identify values that their aspirations to common understandings bring to the fore through the merging of horizons and the creative thinking that dialogue effects. In such a process, tradition is kept on the move and innovation retains an anchorhold, neither dispensing entirely with the other.

Although Spinoza and Van Gogh are interesting figures in themselves, with the foregoing remarks in mind, I have found it fruitful to place them within a broader narrative of the development of Western secular culture from the end of the Middle Ages until the present. In the seventeenth century, that is, Spinoza challenged a great many received opinions and assumptions, and his main ideas were profoundly influential in the reshaping of Western culture and society in the subsequent two centuries. This broad reshaping is what I mean by Modernity. It did not come about solely because of Spinoza, but it is as if his thinking rang true to what many people realized was under way but could not face so comprehensively and directly. Instead, for the most part, they recoiled in violent hostility, captivated by what repelled them. Spinoza's new ways of thinking about reason, religion and nature also strongly promoted the development of science, and, in addition, he introduced highly influential, critical re-appraisals of the Bible that by and by promoted secularism and democracy, which he thought the best form of government, however radical that idea was in his own times. As the standard historical narrative tells us, the high value accorded to reason in the advancement of science during the eighteenth-century Enlightenment provoked the Romantic reaction in the early nineteenth century, calling for a re-integration with nature from which science, technology and analytic reason had alienated great numbers of newly urbanized people. The Romantic protest against the alienations caused by industrialization was directed especially against the kind of scientific rationality that Spinoza promoted, and yet, the Romantic movement also drew heavily on a further aspect of Spinoza's legacy. That is, in rejecting traditional ideas about God's transcendence, Spinoza emphasized the immanence of the divine agency in nature through the generative process of *natura naturans*, in contrast to the outward, material structures that we observe as *natura naturata*.[32] The Romantic movement likewise sought to promote the vital, generative processes of nature as a means of healing the alienations that were laying waste to the lives of great numbers of people under the infernal regime of industrial production combined with *laissez-faire* capitalism. The restorative powers of *natura naturans* then assumed a quasi-religious efficacy, the "natural supernaturalism" described in the later nineteenth century by Thomas Carlyle[33] who, as it happened, was much influenced by Spinoza and was enthusiastically read by Van Gogh.

Modernity, then, entailed a re-thinking of what was meant by God, Reason and Nature, and Spinoza played a central role in this re-thinking process, which unfolded during the subsequent two centuries and reached a crisis point at the end of the nineteenth century. During those centuries, Christianity remained a significant cultural force, even as a range of dissenting opinions – agnosticism and atheism amongst them – were increasingly heard, as secularism gradually relegated religion, at least in theory, to the private sphere. The Reformation had insisted on God's unmediated and inscrutable transcendence, and the new science by and large concurred in order to concentrate on "secondary causes", which is to say, how the material world actually works. And so, the Reformation and the new science combined to set the stage for a new emphasis[34] on the satisfactions and duties of ordinary life. An increased understanding and control of the material world were, for practical purposes, sufficiently sustaining without the extra value that religion might add (if any). By the later nineteenth century, Christianity then found itself confronted also by Darwin's radically disenchanting narrative of origins which has become, today "the only shared metanarrative among educated people of all cultures that we have", as Robert N. Bellah says.[35] Romantic views of nature also found themselves challenged by the Darwinian view of nature as ravin in tooth and claw, cruelly indifferent to wishful ideas about restored organic unity as an antidote to the woes of industrialization. In short, Modernism emerged by way of a failure of confidence in whatever residual assumptions about God, Reason and Nature had provided anchorage for a belief in progress, liberal values, bourgeois confidence and some sense of shared foundations and humanizing good intentions. Not surprisingly, this failure of confidence was accompanied by a loss of bearings, the absence of norms that Durkheim, writing at the time, described as *anomie*. In one sense, in supplying an antidote to an increasingly mechanized and commercialized society, Modernism remains an inheritor of the Romantic quest for deep, authentic experience of nature as a source of renewal. The Romantic re-visioning did not, however, do much to stem people's appetite for mass produced consumer goods, and the material gratifications supplied by industrial production proved, by and large, to be more captivating than contemplating the sublime. Nonetheless, for Clement Greenberg and Frederik Jameson,[36] amongst others, Modernism is best thought of as a highly creative, post-Romantic reaction against mass commodification and cultural alienation. To this end, the characteristic self-reflexiveness, experimentation with styles, obliqueness, and difficulty by means of which a great many Modernist works from Joyce to Proust and Picasso call attention to the process of their own fabrication, are deliberately designed to set art apart from the commercialized and commodified world of easy, off-the-shelf accessibility. Brian McHale[37] explains that Modernist writers (and, by extension, other artists) addressed the cultural crisis with which they were faced by exploring alternative ways of knowing and understanding, so that their main concerns were epistemological. By contrast, for postmodernist writers today, words create a world rather than seek access to it, and art therefore has an ontological rather than an epistemological function, which is to say, it is not concerned with the recovery of values in the same way as are the High Modernists. Terry Eagleton[38] argues along similar lines that Modernism took for granted that "realism was still dominant" in the "cultural establishment" (66) which Modernist art then undertook to disrupt in order to re-shape values that must be fought for rather than received. Modernism "was old enough to remember a time when there were foundations to human existence, and was still reeling from the shock of their being kicked rudely away" (57). By contrast, postmodernism "feels no dizzying abyss beneath its feet" (58) and is dismissive of questions having to do with foundations, stable values and the like. Consequently, though the High Modernists saw themselves by and large as labouring within a fragmented tradition, they had not given up on recovering whatever pearls of great price lay concealed under the rubble. From the early Impressionists to *Finnegan's Wake*, a great variety of Modernist strategies were directed to engaging anyone who was up for the challenge of actively re-fashioning authentic values from the prevailing detritus. That this appeal was elitist is a fair criticism. By contrast, postmodernism de-emphasizes the difference between high and popular culture, finding gratification instead in sheer variety and in performance for its own sake. This liberated free-for-all promotes an egalitarian, multi-cultural, anti-hierarchical diversity, which is to the good, even though, especially in the present age of instant mass communication without adequately sustaining personal contact, it is dogged by its own shadow, namely, a widespread rootlessness such as has now reached epidemic proportions, as the Surgeon General points out.

I have suggested that Spinoza saw in advance how Modernity would unfold. As far as Vincent van Gogh is concerned, I want to suggest that in engaging with the cultural crisis out of which Modernism was born, his paintings and letters recapitulate the main trajectory of the developments set in motion by Spinoza from the period of the Reformation and the Scientific Revolution until his own day. In his life and work, Van Gogh re-enacted the main phases of that unfolding, and in doing so he felt the full weight of the cultural cross-currents and paradoxes that shaped the crises of his own cultural phase. As with other Modernist artists, he produced work that deliberately resisted commodification even as, paradoxically, he depended on the capitalization of the art market for its promotion. In his letters, he repeatedly denounces the greed, bad taste and pandering of art dealers, but he also makes plans with his art dealer brother Theo to develop much the same kind of dealership himself. Throughout his career he was a traditional realist, insisting that his work should be accessible to ordinary people, even if, paradoxically, he also "tortured the form" in the new Symbolist mode, as Theo wrote, to produce something more challenging and to express more effectively the concerns of a world where traditional realism was insufficient to represent the crisis of the times. And although he knew about *anomie* all too well from personal experience, he also struggled to express himself in ways that would touch on the "infinite", in order to enrich ordinary life with something of eternal value beyond the limits of art. In this undertaking, he embraced, but then discarded, the orthodox religion of his pastor father, going on to explore the promises and benefits of Enlightenment reason and Romantic nature before turning to the aesthetic and to the self-reflexivity of the work of art as the best means of showing us how better to live and relate to one another. At the end, he decided that the aesthetic was insufficient, as he directed his attention to a further, more encompassing good – a new religion that he thought was imminent and about to emerge. Although it would offer something akin to the revelation provided by a work of art, it would go beyond art and transfigure it.

In the present cultural phase, marked by information overload, constant distraction, facile scepticism and the increased isolation of people imprisoned on a treadmill of fetishized competition and delusive individualism, *anomie* remains a threatening force, abetted by its favourite progeny – meaningless-ness and self-destruction. In such a context, the recovery of narratives that might enable the restoration of some adequate bearings and shared values re-quires patient enquiry, a tolerance of complexity and an openness to dialogue. Networks of scholarly enquiry and dialogical exchange already exist across many fields, occupations and walks of life, and in the following chapters I attempt, in the spirit of these other enquiries, to throw some new light on the writings of Spinoza and Van Gogh and thereby to suggest why the narrative in which their work plays a part is significant for the possibilities of religious or spiritual experience and discourse today.

Notes

1 See Robert N. Bellah, "Religious Pluralism and Religious Truth" in *The Robert Bellah Reader*, eds. Robert N. Bellah and Steven M. Tipton (Durham and London: Duke University Press, 2006), pp. 476–7.

2 The late A. D. Nuttall cited this example in conversation, mentioning that he in-tended to use it in something he was writing. I have been unable to determine if he did so.

3 Robert Frost, "Fire and Ice".

4 Merlin Donald, *Origins of the Modern Mind. Three Stages in the Evolution of Cul-ture and Cognition* (Cambridge, MA: Harvard University Press, 1991). Page num-bers are cited in the text.

5 See, for instance, Maryanne Wolf, *Reader, Come Home. The Reading Brain in a Digital World* (New York: Harper Collins, 2018); D. L. Ulin, *The Lost Art of Reading: Why Books Matter in a Distracted Time* (Seattle, Washington: Sasquatch Books, 2010); Nicholas Carr, *The Shallows: What the Internet Is Doing to Our Brains* (New York: W. W. Norton, 2010).
6 "Religious Pluralism and Religious Truth", pp. 476–7.
7 Donald, *Origins of the Modern Mind*, p. 40.
8 Donald, *Origins of the Modern Mind*, pp. 162 ff.; Robert N. Bellah, *Religion in Human Evolution: From the Paleolithic to the Axial Age* (Harvard: Harvard University Press, 2011), pp. 19 ff.
9 I deal with this topic more fully in *Dialogue in the Digital Age* (London and New York: Routledge, 2021), pp. 13, 22.
10 See Karl Jaspers, *The Origin and Goal of History*, trans. Michael Bullock (London: Routledge and Kegan Paul, 1953); *The Origins and Diversity of Axial Age Civilizations*, ed. S. N. Eisenstadt (Albany: State University of New York Press, 1986); *The Axial Age and its Consequences*, ed. Robert N. Bellah and Hans Joas (Cambridge, MA: Harvard University Press, 2012).
11 See *Dialogue in the Digital Age*, p. 91, on dialogue and the full range of our communication skills.
12 See *Totality and Infinity. An Essay on Exteriority*, trans. Alphonso Lingis (Pittsburgh: Duquesne University Press, 1969), pp. 79 ff.
13 On the merging of horizons, see Hans Georg Gadamer, *Truth and Method*, translation revised by Joel Weinsheimer and Donald G. Marshall (London: Bloomsbury Academic, 2013; first published, 1975), pp. 282–94, 317, 382. On dialogue being more than an exchange of opinions, see David Bohm, *On Dialogue* (London: Routledge, 2013), pp. 21, 51, 52. On knowledge, the body and commitment, see Michael Polanyi, *Personal Knowledge. Towards a Post-Critical Philosophy* (New York: Harper and Row, 1964; first published, 1958).
14 On the in-between status of dialogue, see Martin Buber, *I and Thou*, trans. Ronald Gregor Smith (New York: Charles Scribner's Sons, 1958).
15 Terry Eagleton, *The Illusions of Postmodernism* (Oxford: Blackwells, 1996), provides a lively account of the phenomenon, balancing its strengths and weaknesses while offering a generally unfavourable assessment.
16 *La Condition Postmoderne* (1974), trans. Geoff Bennington and Biran Massumi, *The Postmodern Condition. A Report on Knowledge* (Minneapolis: University of Minnesota Press, 1984), p. xxiv.
17 *Our Epidemic of Loneliness and Isolation: The U.S. Surgeon General's Advisory on the Healing Effects of Social Connection and Community* (Office of the U.S. Surgeon General, 2023). Page numbers are cited in the text.
18 Hannah Arendt, "Ideology and Terror: A Novel Form of Government" in *The Origins of Totalitarianism* (New York: Meridian Books, 1958; first published, 1951), pp. 460 ff. While this book was in production, an article in the Guardian, 5 September, 2024, by V. (formerly Eve Ensler), "The forces of loneliness can cause political instability. And threaten democracy", made the same point connecting the Surgeon General's report to totalitarianism through Hannah Arendt.
19 Robert Reich, "How Wealth Inequality Spiraled out of Control," *RobertReich.org*, Wednesday, 3 November, 2021.
20 Émile Durkheim, *The Division of Labour in Society*, trans. George Simpson (New York: Free Press, 1964; first published, 1893), p. 413; *Suicide. A Study in Sociology*, trans. John A. Spaulding and George Simpson (London: Routledge, 2002); first published, 1897). See Marco Orrù, *Anomie. History and Meanings* (Boston: Allen and Unwin, 1987), pp. 104 ff., on Durkheim's "Pathological Anomie".

21 See *The Legacy of Anomie Theory*, ed. Freda Adler and William S. Laufer, intro. Robert K. Merton, Advances in Criminological Theory, Vol. 6 (New Brunswick and London: Transaction Publishers, 2000; first published, 1995; *Automation, Alienation, and Anomie*, ed. Simon Mareson (New York: Harper and Row, 1970).
22 Charles Taylor, *A Secular Age* (Harvard: Harvard University Press, 2007), p. 595.
23 Walter Benjamin, "Capitalism as Religion," in *Selected Writings*, Vol. 1, trans. Rodney Livingstone (London: Belknap Harvard Press, 1996; first published, 1921), pp. 288–91.
24 See Malise Ruthven, *The Divine Supermarket: Travels in Search of the Soul of America* (London: Chatto and Windus, 1989).
25 See Charles Taylor, *A Secular Age*, pp. 594 ff.
26 Van Gogh's letters provide the best evidence, but his literary accomplishment has not been sufficiently acknowledged. I attempt to address this omission in *The Letters of Vincent van Gogh. A Critical Study* (Edmonton: Athabasca University Press, 2014); *My Own Portrait in Writing. Self-Fashioning in the Letters of Vincent van Gogh* (Edmonton: Athabasca University Press, 2015); *Reading Vincent van Gogh. A Thematic Guide to the Letters* (Edmonton: Athabasca University Press, 2016).
27 See Karl Jaspers, *The Origin and Goal of History* (New Haven: Yale University Press, 1953), pp.1–25. Yehuda Elkana, "The Emergence of Second-Order Thinking in Classical Greece," and S. N. Eisenstadt, "The Axial Age Breakthroughs – Their Characteristics and Origins," in *The Origins and Diversity of Axial Age Civilizations*, ed. S. N. Eisenstadt, pp. 58 ff.; 5 ff.
28 See Patrick Grant, *Literature and the Discovery of Method in the English Renaissance* (London: Macmillan, 1985), pp. 11 ff.
29 Charles Taylor, *A Secular Age*, p. 772.
30 Similar points are made by Byung-Chul Han, *The Disappearance of Rituals*, trans. Daniel Steurer (Cambridge: Polity Press, 2020), pp. 44 ff.
31 See, for instance, Northrop Frye, *The Modern Century* (Toronto: Oxford University Press, 1991), p. 119.
32 For example, Coleridge draws directly on Spinoza's distinction between *natura naturans* and *natura naturata*. See *The Philosophical Lectures of Samuel Taylor Coleridge*, ed. Kathleen Coburn (London: The Pilate Press, Ltd., 1949), p. 370.
33 See Thomas Carlyle, *Sartor Resartus*, ed. Kerry McSweeny and Peter Sabor (Oxford: Oxford University Press, 2008; first published, 1987), pp. 193 ff.
34 See Charles Taylor, *Sources of the Self. The Making of the Modern Identity* (Cambridge, MA: Harvard University Press, 1989), pp. 211 ff.; *A Secular Age*, p. 179.
35 Bellah, *Religion in Human Evolution*, p. 600.
36 Clement Greenberg, *Art and Culture. Critical Essays* (Boston: Beacon Press, 1961), pp. 3–33; Fredric Jameson, "Reification and Utopia in Mass Culture," *Social Text* 1 (Winter, 1979), cited in Terry Eagleton, *Against the Grain: Essays 1975-1985* (London: Verso, 1986), p. 194.
37 Brian McHale, *Postmodernist Fiction* (London: Routledge, 1987).
38 Terry Eagleton, *After Theory* (New York: Basic Books, 2003). Page numbers are cited in the text.

2 Spinoza's Bad Dream

Baruch Spinoza (1632–1677) was an outsider without social status, money or standard academic training in philosophy, but his work sent such shockwaves through the whole of Europe that what he lacked in social status he made up for in notoriety. In effect, Spinoza had drawn up a blueprint for Modernity, but his ideas were so challenging to received opinion at the time that they were met with an all but universal repudiation, fuelled by alarm, consternation and fear.

As I mentioned in the previous chapter, by Modernity I mean a broad, increasingly secularizing trajectory of Western civilization in the wake of the Scientific Revolution and the Protestant Reformation. Spinoza grasped the implications of these revolutionary cultural movements with a singular lucidity, unmatched in his own time. As with the Protestant reformers, the new scientists of the sixteenth and seventeenth centuries placed a strong emphasis on God's transcendence, so that their pious acknowledgement of the special revelation contained in the Bible allowed them to maintain an orthodox observance while they got on with separating religion from the practical scientific work of exploring the laws of nature. Their focus was on "secondary causes" (the way things work in the physical world), rather than "primary causes" (the first principles held to explain the design and purpose of the created world as a whole).[1]

In an analogous way, by rejecting the mediating agency of the church as a bridge between heaven and earth, the main Reformers insisted on God's transcendence, while also placing a special, intensified emphasis on the duties of ordinary life. The beginnings of Modernity are marked by this shared, levelling spirit of scepticism, empiricism, and this-worldliness that fundamentally challenged the Axial Age, metaphysically based, hierarchically ordered view of the universe that had by and large prevailed during the Middle Ages. Gradually – however imperfectly and unevenly – enlightened reasonableness, democracy, secularization, universal rights and religious toleration took shape in Europe during the centuries after Spinoza's death in 1677. Although he would have been surprised by a great deal of what the modern world has become, he had discerned with remarkable clarity the lineaments of a radical

DOI: 10.4324/9781003546856-2

reordering of thought and values that was to define the modern phase of Western European society and culture.

Spinoza in outline

The main lines of Spinoza's system of thought came to him surprisingly early in his life, almost as a single, comprehensive set of themes and ideas.[2] His life's work then was a deepening and intensifying of that first, comprehensive set of understandings rather than a lateral extension of it. It is as if he sank mineshafts instead of searching for treasure abroad.

In Portuguese, Spinoza's given name was Bento, in Hebrew, Baruch, and he used the Latin form, Benedictus, when he expounded his philosophical views in writing. These variations in his name can help to clarify some key facts about his life.[3] As the son of immigrant Sephardic Jews in Amsterdam, Bento spoke Portuguese, the language of his parents' land of origin. In Amsterdam, the Sephardic Jewish community made a significant contribution to the city's growing prosperity through trade and commerce. This contribution was valued and the Jewish community was accepted, even though with reservations. Cautionary measures were taken to limit its influence on the general population, especially where religion was concerned.

As an official member of the Jewish community, Bento was referred to as Baruch, and, as part of his education, he acquired, amongst other things, a reading knowledge of Hebrew and of the Hebrew scriptures.[4] After the death of his father, he left school and helped to run the family business. He had little interest in trade and commerce, but during his visits to the Bourse he encountered a cross section of the various groups of dissident thinkers who were thriving – or, at least, were tolerated – in Amsterdam at the time.[5] Broadly, these unorthodox protesters comprised assorted Socinians, Anabaptists, Armenians, Mennonites, Quakers and Collegiants, amongst other fringe figures. Despite their diversity, they were held together by the high value they placed on religious liberty, toleration and freedom of enquiry. Not surprisingly, they incurred the disapproval of the Calvinist ecclesiastical authorities, by whom they were frequently harassed. Nonetheless, as Jonathan Israel writes of the group as a whole, "nowhere else in the Western world could even remotely rival it".[6]

In his early twenties (exactly when is not clear) Spinoza fell under the influence of Franciscus van Enden, a teacher who had once been a Jesuit but was expelled (twice) from the order. Van Enden tried running a gallery and a bookshop before setting up a private academy in his house, where he taught Latin and promoted a non-sectarian educational programme that was anti-hierarchical and anti-authoritarian.[7] Under Van Enden's influence, "Benedictus" began to take shape, and, as if to emphasize the transition, Baruch was expelled from the Jewish community, following an official pronouncement of excommunication, or *cherem*, delivered in 1656, when Spinoza was 23.

The *cherem* was so severe as to cause a reader of it today to wonder at how deep a nerve Spinoza had struck. It is not clear exactly what offence he gave, but there are indications that he denied the immortality of the soul and that God is an omnipotent, transcendent creator. He also held that the Pentateuch was not written by Moses, and that after the dissolution of the Jewish state as the Bible describes it, the law is no longer binding on Jews. There were precedents within his own tradition for some of these ideas, for instance in the writings of Ibn Ezra, Juan de Prado and Uriel da Costa, amongst others.[8] But Spinoza's adventures into the free-thinking world of the Collegiants and Van Enden (with whom he probably had contact before the *cherem*) must have contributed to the sense that he was a special liability – indeed, a danger – to the Jewish community as a whole.[9] This is especially so because his opinions were offensive to Christians as well as to Jews, and the Jewish community had to be concerned not to harbour someone who held inflammatory opinions that would also offend the Calvinist Regents of Amsterdam. In short, Spinoza had to be expelled as forcefully and unequivocally as possible to make it clear that his opinions were as unacceptable to Jews as to Christians. The *cherem* did what was required. For his part, Spinoza seems to have walked away without recriminations, cooly observing that "they do not force me to do anything that I would not have done of my own accord if I did not dread scandal".[10]

Spinoza's whereabouts during the following five years are uncertain, but in the summer of 1661, he moved to Rijnsburg, a village close to Leiden where there was a university in which he might have been interested. Two years later, he moved to Voorburg, near The Hague, and, finally, in 1670, to The Hague, where he died in 1677.

In the years leading up to his move to Rijnsburg, Spinoza probably worked on the *Treatise on the Emendation of the Intellect*, in which he discusses method. A draft of the *Treatise* existed in 1662,[11] and Spinoza would likely have written it in the years directly leading up to that date. He did not complete it, however, and he moved on, instead, to the *Short Treatise on God, Man and His Well-Being*, in which he explored metaphysics and morality, topics that would become central to his main work, the *Ethics*. As Edwin Curley points out, the *Short Treatise* contains reflections on ideas not fully explored in the otherwise more complete *Ethics*, such as God's causality of the finite and the distinction between *natura naturans* and *natura naturata*.[12] In 1663, as a way of laying the groundwork for publishing of his own theories, Spinoza wrote an expository account of Descartes' *Principles of Philosophy*, together with an appendix, *Metaphysical Thoughts*. These are the only works published under his own name during his lifetime.

It is difficult to determine when Spinoza began working on the *Ethics*. He had been exploring its central themes from as far back as we can trace his thinking, including the opinions that brought the *cherem* upon him. Consequently, there is a substantial overlap between the *Short Treatise* and his later work, confirming the point I made earlier that Spinoza's development charts a deepening and intensification of his enquiry rather than a lateral expansion of it. As the correspondence makes clear,[13] drafts of the first part of the *Ethics* were in circulation amongst friends in 1661, and he had finished a complete early version of it by 1665. He realized that the *Ethics* would be inflammatory, so he set the manuscript aside in order to write the *Theological-Political Treatise*. His plan was to pre-empt objections to the *Ethics* by explaining the differences between religion and philosophy, and in that light to make a case for freedom of expression in philosophy. He anticipated that the *Theological-Political Treatise* would also be controversial, and as a precaution, he did not publish it under his own name, and he invented a fictional press and place of publication.

As it turned out, when the *Theological-Political Treatise* appeared in 1670, it created a scandal far beyond Spinoza's expectations, eliciting a storm of repudiations and personal vilification. Far from clearing a path towards publication of the *Ethics*, the *Theological-Political Treatise* all but ensured that it would be impossible for Spinoza to publish the book he considered his main work.[14] Still, during the following five years, he continued to work on the *Ethics* and in 1675 a version was ready for the press. Prudently, he decided not to proceed with publication and the book remained unpublished until after his death.

As Henri Bergson says, the *Ethics* sets in operation an "intricate machinery" with the "crushing power" of "an armoured dreadnaught"[15] aimed at traditional metaphysics, as well as traditional concepts of a creator God, divine providence and free will. Throughout, Spinoza's arguments are clear and unflinchingly logical, while at the same time managing, somehow, to convey a charged undercurrent of passionate conviction. Antonio Negri describes the *Ethics* as "a philosophical *Bildungsroman*", and commentators such as Gilles Deleuze and Karl Jaspers draw attention to a creative energy that transforms the text, turning it into something a great deal more than its constituent arguments.[16] Entering into the world of the *Ethics* can feel rather like going into a hall of mirrors where everything is geometrically fashioned with a high degree of precision, and yet the effect is also strangely magical and disorienting, as one's habitual expectations and ways of seeing are thrown into a dazzling confusion that remains, at the same time, crystal clear.

At the time of his death, Spinoza was writing the *Political Treatise*. A substantial amount survives, including an incomplete section on democracy, the form of government that Spinoza favoured. The incomplete text, as well as a *Compendium of Hebrew Grammar* was published posthumously, and there is a collection of letters (84, in Curley's edition of *The Collected Works*) which throw considerable extra light on several aspects of Spinoza's thinking.

Unlike, say, Thomas Aquinas and Emmanuel Kant, Spinoza did not develop his main arguments in the *Ethics* in exhaustive detail, and because his arguments are so concentrated, the *Ethics* is a difficult and challenging book. A great amount of scholarship is given over to teasing out what the author meant, or might have meant, on a wide range of points on which he did not expand. Still, the main principles can readily enough be summarized.

The *Ethics* begins by describing God as the source of all that is, and ends by describing the intellectual love of God as the supreme human achievement. Spinoza defined God philosophically as a single Substance, and he rejects the Biblical creator God as an invention designed to enforce obedience by playing on people's fears and superstitions, mainly for political purposes. By contrast, Spinoza argues that the world is produced, or generated, by necessity and is governed by the laws of cause and effect to which science gives us access. Rational thinking can therefore enable us to have an adequate knowledge of God,[17] in contrast to the deluded anthropomorphisms and superstitions of the Biblical version of a creator who stands outside a world that was brought into being by divine fiat, and which might not have existed had God chosen otherwise. Spinoza does not say that there is no truth in the Bible; only that whatever truth the Bible teaches is accessible to reason, the main example being, simply, that we should love God and our neighbour.

Spinoza goes on to explain that reason also enables us to know that God does not have purposes, and therefore there are no "final causes", just as there are no miracles[18] and no providential design. God can be described as free insofar as God operates without constraint, even though by necessity.[19] By contrast, all that is not God operates within limits, through the chains of cause and effect that science investigates. Spinoza's famous declaration, "Deus sive natura" ("God, *or* Nature"),[20] is the topic of much discussion, but the main point is that although God's creative power (*natura naturas*) is not reducible to the "modes" by which that power is manifest in the material world (*natura naturata*), nonetheless, God is immanent and therefore inseparable from the laws of nature.

The ethical and political consequences of Spinoza's radical revision of traditional theology were all too clear to his detractors, who saw that in dispensing with miracles, sin, hell, heaven, he also dispensed with accountability, after we die, for our transgressions while we were alive on earth. How would people behave if they thought there were no rewards or punishments in the afterlife, no checks on whatever criminal acts they could get away with because of the all-too-evident deficiencies of justice on earth? Admittedly, Spinoza argued for the survival after death of a certain aspect of the human mind,[21] even though he also held that the soul dies with the body, which has a limited duration. Because the mind grasps things *sub specie aeternitatis*, it is not limited by duration or by temporal change. And yet, as Spinoza's detractors saw, this philosophical view of immortality is far removed from the kinds of belief engendered by traditional religion about rewards and punishments based on our personal accountability.

Spinoza's critique of traditional religion was underpinned by the fact that he regarded the Bible not as a unique, supernaturally inspired sacred text, but as a book – or collection of books – produced in the same way as every other book. Again, a strong levelling impulse informs this fundamentally secular reading of the one text widely regarded in the Europe of his day as the only complete, authoritative revelation of God's purposes and directives for our eternal salvation. And so Spinoza realized that he could not reform politics[22] without changing standard views of the Bible, and the bulk of the *Theological-Political Treatise* is given over to a detailed critical analysis of the sacred texts, aimed at effecting a separation of theology and philosophy, in order to promote religious toleration and freedom of expression.

One main argument in the *Theological-Political Treatise* is that the authority of the Bible depends on the fact that people are fundamentally susceptible to fear and hope. The prophets, who were not philosophers, had vivid imaginations which they used to manipulate this susceptibility in order to exercise control and to consolidate the authority of the state, from which the religious cult is inseparable. In short, imagination is the main means by which Biblical religion is promoted, and through imagination, superstition is all the more readily stimulated, in order then to be manipulated. Judged by the standards of reasoned enquiry (of which Spinoza's Biblical criticism is itself an example), the mysteries, miracles and anthropomorphisms of the Bible are discovered to be obfuscations, the main purpose of which is to ensure obedience. If we seek in the Bible for a message conforming to reason, it turns out to be simple: "obedience to God consists only in the love of your neighbor" (II, 258). Spinoza describes this teaching as "universal" emphasizing that it is not confined to the claims of any particular religious group. In short, "natural knowledge is divine" (II, 77), and "[true] religion is to follow the laws of Nature" (I, 129). Here, once again, the supernatural is assimilated to the natural, and yet, the extent to which Spinoza naturalized the spiritual as distinct from spiritualizing the natural is not easy to determine, and there are advocates on both sides. As the Romantics discovered, the disenchanting rationalism typical of one aspect of the Enlightenment called for a countervailing appreciation of a divine mystery that is immanent, and Coleridge found this kind of counterbalance especially in Spinoza's *natura naturans.* Later in the nineteenth century, Thomas Carlyle's "natural supernaturalism" describes a similar emphasis,[23] and although Novalis's description of Spinoza as a "god-intoxicated man" is extravagant, it would be misleading to ignore the spiritual dimension of Spinoza's thought, even though it is not easy to pin down.[24] As Edwin Curley says, Spinoza is not a theist in the usual sense of the term but he resented being called an atheist.[25] In a letter, he complains to Henry Oldenburg that the "common people" "never stop accusing me of atheism", and "I am forced to rebut this accusation as well as I can" (II, 14). In a further letter, Lambert van Velthuysen denounces Spinoza "for teaching pure Atheism, by disguised and counterfeit arguments" (II, 385), but Spinoza rejects this, along with other "perversely" constructed accusations against him (II, 388). Again, writing to Henry Oldenburg, he counters a "rumor" that he has tried "to show that there is no God" (II, 459). It has been pointed out that Spinoza's thinking has much in common with Vedanta,[26] and a summary of his main positions would contain few surprises for Vedanta scholars. But Spinoza had no exposure to Indian thought, and in contrast to that traditional body of writing, his work is highly individual, even though drawing on Jewish, Christian and classical sources. As Edwin Curley concludes, "there is no easy way" to label Spinoza's religious position. On the one hand, it is incorrect to classify him as an atheist "if that term is taken to imply the rejection of all belief in God and all religion generally". On the other hand, "to regard him as a kind of theist is to stretch the boundaries of theism" (II, 49).

Metaphysics, mystery and double reading

Spinoza's blurring of the boundaries between secular and sacred remains highly pertinent to any consideration of a viable spirituality today. As Charles Taylor argues, traditional dogmatic prescriptions from positions of traditional ecclesiastical authority can now best be validated by how effectively they enable an enhanced understanding of the implicit sacredness of ordinary things and human relationships within the over-arching, encompassing mystery. In this order of priorities, traditional religious dogma will rediscover its symbolic efficacy as distinct, though not separate from its prescriptive formulations. With this view in mind, Taylor concludes that we are "just at the beginning of a new age of religious searching, whose outcome no one can foresee".[27] He also argues that the conditions for this search were laid down by the development of secularism and by a new evaluation of the immanence of the creative process. I will want to suggest that Spinoza's philosophy did much to initiate and describe how these developments took shape, and I will come back to this point by and by.

For now, I want to return to Spinoza's description of true religion as loving your neighbour according to reason and the laws of nature. The reduction of religion to this simple moral precept was profoundly unsettling to received opinion, and its broader historical impact can be grasped if we consider Spinoza's other, analogous demystifications of traditional views of transcendence in the field of theology (a creator God, providence), epistemology (traditional metaphysics, universals) and politics (monarchy, and social hierarchy as divinely instituted). That is, the core precept about loving your neighbour is part of a much more extensive and radical system of thought, as the *Ethics* especially helps us to see.

As I have mentioned, Spinoza begins the *Ethics* by arguing that there is only one Substance, which he identifies as God. He defines Substance as "what is in itself and is conceived through itself, i.e., that whose concept does not require the concept of another thing, from which it must be formed" (I, 408). The single Substance has attributes, by which Spinoza means "what the intellect perceives of a substance, as constituting its essence." (I, 408). An attribute is the underlying nature of what a thing is, and God is "a substance consisting of an infinity of attributes, of which each one expresses an eternal and infinite essence" (I, 408). As human beings, we know only two such attributes, namely thought and extension – which is to say, mind and body.

Spinoza goes on to argue that there cannot be two or more substances "*of the same nature or attribute*" (I, 411). This is so because an attribute is the essence of a substance, and a substance would not be self-identical if it had more than one essence. Moreover, because substance, by definition, is not formed from another substance, "its essence necessarily involves existence, *or* it pertains to its nature to exist" (I, 412). "If you deny this", Spinoza states, "conceive, if you can, that God does not exist." That is, God's essence must "involve existence" and it is "absurd" to think otherwise. The prestidigitation is complete, as Spinoza draws on the old-fashioned language of substances and on the "ontological argument" (especially associated with Anselm) claiming that a perfect being exists because existence is a condition of perfection; consequently, we cannot conceive of a perfect being without allowing that such a being exists. "By cause of itself", Spinoza states at the outset, "I understand that whose essence involves existence, *or* that whose nature cannot be conceived except as existing" (I, 408).

As elsewhere in the *Ethics*, Spinoza assumes, as Roger Scruton says, that "relations of dependence in the world are intelligible as logical relations between ideas" [28], and Spinoza makes this claim especially clear in his innovative definition of the mind as the idea of the body (I, 494). That is, he argues that the idea of a body and the body itself are a single thing expressed by way of the two attributes of thought and extension. As with all the attributes (of which God has an infinite number), thought and extension are independent of one another, but mind-body dualism is, for Spinoza, not dualism at all. Rather, a single entity is being described from two different viewpoints. It follows that our ideas about a particular body give us real knowledge of the body, and, as Scruton says, logical relations really do correspond to how things naturally exist in the world.

As is often pointed out, Spinoza's definitions and the propositions deriving from them are frequently not as self-evident as he assumes, and we might wonder about the consequences of this rather significant fact for his thinking as a whole. One challenge for a reader is to sort out the degree to which Spinoza's analyses have a persuasive force that makes a provisional acceptance of his more dubious definitions worthwhile. That is, we find ourselves asking if the comprehensive power of his vision compensates for our objections to the premises on which it is based. As Steven Nadler says, "perhaps, then, we should look at the entire structure of the *Ethics* as simply Spinoza's attempt to show what can be derived from some basic but not necessarily true starting point", so that the definitions are "'proven' by their consequences".[29] Yet, we should also be mindful that placing his definitions in parenthesis in this way runs contrary to Spinoza's own conviction that they are true. Karl Jaspers helpfully addresses this problem by pointing out that "metaphysics as a hypothesis of the world as a whole is meaningless" because it is "impossible to start from a source, however concretely conceived, in order to express all things in one". That is, the whole of which we are a part cannot be observed except from some point of view within it. Being remains an "encompassing" mystery, and Spinoza's one Substance (which he perplexingly says cannot actually be called "one" because enumeration is itself a limitation) with its infinite attributes remains beyond our grasp, despite his claim that we can have an adequate knowledge of it. In this context, Jaspers argues that Spinoza's frequent reliance on metaphors shows that his metaphysics, like all metaphysics, serves "to express the mystery itself. It is a discourse addressed to the mystery, purporting to illuminate it, not to explain it."[30]

Jaspers goes on to emphasize the existential dimension of Spinoza's thought, and in so doing, brings us into the hinterland between philosophy and literature. This is the domain also of much modern literary theory, which is especially concerned to discover the latent metaphoricity of philosophical discourse purporting to be exclusively conceptual. The strong forbear of this line of thinking is Nietzsche, who proposed that "every great philosophy" is "a personal confession of its originator, a type of involuntary and unaware memoir"[31] that rests always on "a shifting texture of figurative language".[32] Gilles Deleuze offers a heavily theorized reading of Spinoza along Nietzschean lines, arguing that in a typically Nietzschean manner, Spinoza "denounces all the falsifications of life, all the values in the name of which we disparage life." By contrast, the key to Spinoza's enduring influence is that he "projects an image of the positive, affirmative life". He "believed only in joy, and in vision", and, like Nietzsche, "wanted only to inspire, to waken, to reveal". Deleuze proposes that there is, therefore, a "double reading" of Spinoza, the first aspect of which is systematic, and the second, literary. For the most part, the systematic reading is a vehicle for the literary, which is to say, for the "immediate, unprepared encounter" by which we "receive a sudden illumination", and which marks us as true Spinozists, as a great many artists and non-philosophers have discovered.[33]

Deleuze's Nietzschean commentary makes Spinoza sound a lot more like Blake than the rationalist that Spinoza held himself to be. Nonetheless, Deleuze does a real service by highlighting a certain visionary intensity burning beneath the cool surfaces of Spinoza's carefully chiseled prose. And although he runs the risk of having a chaotic creative energy over-ride Spinoza's power of reasoned demonstration, Deleuze highlights a dimension in the *Ethics* that has, whether recognized or not, contributed a great deal to the fascination that the book continues to exercise on readers. Scruton, Nadler and Jaspers (amongst others) also draw attention to this elusive combination of analytical rigour and affective, visionary power.

Spinoza himself would have reservations, however. Although he held traditional metaphysics in contempt, he remained a metaphysician, and he did not regard metaphysics as a species of metaphor imaginatively representing an encompassing mystery that is more properly evoked rather than scientifically described. For Spinoza, reason prevails and many of his carefully argued positions have become part of our everyday, secular assumptions and understandings. These include his critique of religion, his promotion of democracy and toleration, his separation of theology from philosophy, his re-evaluation of nature as a creative and productive power without purpose or "final cause", his promotion of the scientific spirit, together with a levelling impulse towards "a *common plane of immanence*" (as Deleuze says) within which we belong equally and which entails "a mode of living, a way of life"[34] based on reason. All this, together with the disputes to which it gives rise, is a tool kit of ideas that are indispensable to a modern secular and democratic way of life, and which, for Spinoza, were based on the idea of a single Substance to which reason directs us.

Here, we might pause to notice that in making metaphysical claims that are now mostly discarded, Spinoza joins thinkers such as Plato, Augustine, Boethius and Aquinas, amongst many others whose work is based on premodern premises and assumptions. These writers often remain interesting today because we still feel engaged by the insights they provide into many aspects of common experience. In Spinoza's case, however, there is a further complexity because his rational, "geometric" demonstrations, challenged the assumptions of a great many of his contemporaries, even as he clung to some old-fashioned metaphysical ways of thinking. The ensuing tension in his writing sometimes provokes him to express frustration, as he berates recalcitrant readers who are insufficiently able to negotiate the challenges his arguments present. Even in a work as formal and austere as the *Ethics*, an authorial voice intrudes, often expressing a personally felt exasperation. This voice can be peremptory, ("them I dismiss" [I, 421]), patronizing ("I believe this will be clear even to those who are only moderately attentive" [I, 419]), dismissive ("I shall waste no time in refuting this absurdity" [I, 439]), impatient ("But enough of this" [I, 445]) and irritated ("*I would hardly have believed it had been propounded by so great a Man*" [I, 596]). In a telling moment, he even refers to "our cumbersome Geometric order" (I, 555), as if acknowledging the limitations of his preferred style of demonstration. In the more directly polemical *Theological-Political Treatise*, expressions of irritation are a great deal more vigorous: "a ridiculous way of confessing their ignorance" (II, 157); "How shameful" (II, 159); "Each is insane" (II, 272); "Who but someone desperate and mad" (II, 280); "But this is childish" (II, 317) and so on. In the letters, personal opinions are often expressed with a surprising vehemence, and, clearly, when his patience was tried, Spinoza did not suffer fools gladly. And so, although he proposed that his metaphysical principles are self-evident, he also realized how his demonstrations might not be as persuasive as he might wish, perhaps not least because he also realized something of their further, anti-metaphysical implications. In this context, it is worth also noticing that his arguments, besides being often difficult, are sometimes insufficiently resolved, a fact that might have been discouraging not only to readers but maybe also to himself. For instance, in his opening arguments in the *Ethics* he states that "there exists only one substance" (I, 416), and elsewhere, he argues that because God, as Substance, is "*absolutely infinite*" and "*indivisible*", it follows "most clearly" that God is "unique" (I, 420). And yet, in a letter to Jarig Jelles, Spinoza insists that "God can only very improperly be called one or unique", and "it's certain that someone who calls God one or unique does not have a true idea of God, or is speaking improperly about him". The main reason for this caveat is that number applies only "to finite and determinate bodies", and, therefore, not to God (II, 406). In order, then, to counter the difficulty of imagining the existence of something that does not have a numerical identity, Spinoza assures us that we can conceive what we cannot imagine: "we can't imagine God, but we can indeed understand him" (II, 423). And so, if we allow that God is intelligent, we must also allow that God's intellect "differs from our intellect both as to its essence and as to its existence" (I, 427). Again, concept dissolves into mystery when Spinoza proposes that God has "absolutely infinite attributes" (I, 425), because, given that we know only the two attributes of thought and extension, we cannot imagine what the other attributes might be, let alone picture them as infinite in number. When Tschirnhaus raises the awkward question of why our knowledge is limited to the attributes of thought and extension, Spinoza does not answer. And when Schuller asks the same question, Spinoza can only reassert that "the human Mind cannot achieve knowledge of any other attribute of God beyond these" (II, 438). Again, Tschirnhaus wonders if the two attributes have the same status, given that extension is grasped through thought, and, therefore, "the Attribute of thought is held to extend itself much more widely than the other attributes". How can this be, Tschirnhaus wants to know, if "each of the attributes constitutes the Essence of God" (II, 462)? Spinoza does not supply any clarification, and, faced with these complexities, it is a good deal less easy for us to be convinced that we do in fact have "adequate knowledge" of God's essence. It might be argued here that Spinoza is taking a highly restricted view of "adequate", but we are more likely to be impressed by the inadequacy of what we know about God, than the reverse.

Similar sticking points occur in Spinoza's accounts of the foundations of ethical behaviour. For instance, he makes clear that all beings strive to preserve themselves and increase their power, and to that extent, his ethics is based on self-interest: "the supreme law of nature is that each thing strives to preserve its state", and "each individual has a supreme right to do everything it can" (II, 282) to promote its own interests. He then sets out the standard social contract idea that it is in our interest to join forces with others because "*a man who is guided by reason is more free in a state, where he lives according to a common decision*" (I, 587). If people co-operate in establishing a well-regulated social order or "common society" (I, 491), their self-interest will be well served. Spinoza even pushes the self-interest theory in the direction propounded later by John Mandeville, to the effect that some private vices should be encouraged because they promote the public good. And so, in the *Political Treatise*, he declares that certain "common vices" should not be prohibited entirely because they can be "advantageous to the Republic". For example, the rich should be encouraged to be greedy because they will be able to increase their wealth "without disgrace", and will thereby contribute to the public good (II, 599).

And yet, there is also a contrary movement in Spinoza's thinking about ethical behaviour, whereby human perfection is held to consist in bringing others, rather than just ourselves, to a state of shared understanding. In this view, knowledge is not competitive and the good we want for ourselves is not complete unless it "can be enjoyed by all equally." The "*greatest good of those who seek virtue is common to all*" (I, 564), Spinoza writes, and "the good which everyone who seeks virtue wants for himself, he also desires for other men" (I, 565). In light of these complexities, Matthew Stewart suggests that Spinoza's philosophy contains an "esoteric message" which "is aimed for the exclusive fellowship of reason", and Étienne Balibar coins the term "transindividual"[35] to indicate the same transcendence of self-interest in the promotion of the common good. Attempts to explain Spinoza's altruism as merely a further variety of individual gratification do not resolve the conflict in his work between an egoistic moral theory and a "transindividual" impulse to go beyond selfishness in the pursuit of a good that is one and the same for all. I will return to this point later. For now, in Spinoza's view, reason is our best means of access to truth, even though his own superb rationality keeps running up against cross-currents and dilemmas that agitate his thought, infusing it, as Deleuze says, with an "impulse" that makes reading him "an encounter, a passion".[36]

The critique of religion

As I have mentioned, Spinoza naturalizes the supernatural, and in so doing, he demystifies traditional religious claims by re-situating God within the order of nature as science allows us to know it. But it is also important to notice that Spinoza divinizes nature insofar as he regards it as the manifestation of an immanent, creative process that he identifies with God, even while insisting that God is not simply identifiable with the "modes" of material nature as we experience it. His bold declaration, "*deus sive natura*" ("God, *or* Nature") (I, 544), which was published in the Latin edition of the *Ethics* but not in the Dutch translation, emphasizes that the divine and the natural are inseparable. His well-known distinction between *natura naturans* and *natura naturata* goes on to explain that there is a difference between nature as a product (*naturata*) and God's creative energy (*naturans*), and Karl Jaspers suggests that "*deus sive natura*" ("God, *or* Nature") refers to the creative source, *naturans*, rather than to the phenomena (or "modes", Spinoza would say) of material nature that are manifest through the attribute of extension. More recently, Clare Carlisle confirms Jaspers' point: "Spinoza offers *Natura naturans* as, so to speak, an alternative name for God".[37]

The argument that Spinoza used "God" mainly as a stalking horse to promote atheism is easy to make if we concede that he did not dare to declare his atheism openly. We can then interpret his great many references to God as a strategic obfuscation, and it is not possible to disprove that sort of circular argument.[38] ("My master talks with angels" might elicit the question, "How do you know?", to which the circular thinker replies, "Fool, would an angel lie?"). But Spinoza is not like De la Mettrie, for whom the human being is a machine. Rather, for all his trust in analytical reason and respect for the laws of nature, Spinoza's arguments acknowledge a creative, originating source, whether by way of his views on eternity, *natura naturans*, God's infinite attributes, or his assertion that one aspect of the mind is immortal.[39]

Consequently, rather than focussing on Spinoza's denial of the traditional Biblical creator God, it might be helpful to imagine him as displacing the creative source from a vertical axis onto a horizontal one. That is, on the traditional Biblical model, God stands above and outside the world which was brought into being by divine *fiat*. By contrast, Spinoza's God is better imagined as operating along a horizontal axis as a generative power immanent in its manifestations and not free to produce any other effects than those that actually are the case. As we have seen, this re-imagining of the creative process and the divine economy entailed a rejection of traditional ideas about an afterlife with rewards in heaven and suffering in hell. Such beliefs seemed to Spinoza to be superstitions that followed on absurdly anthropomorphic depictions of God and God's vertical transcendence. Hell is merely a scare tactic, a sort of nightmare conjured up by ecclesiastical authorities to control people. By contrast, Spinoza's horizontal model offers a release from the burden of guilt and fear that many people found (as many still do) oppressive and life-denying. And yet, I also want to suggest that Spinoza's own system of thought, as I have now briefly described it, contains its own nightmare scenario, a bad dream anticipating a modern "secular hell", another name for which is *anomie*. Here, yet again, Spinoza was prophetic. Let me explain.

The traditional Christian view is that God created the world *ex nihilo* and divine providence governs the unfolding of events towards a final ingathering which will be the consummation of God's plan. By contrast, for Spinoza, it did not make sense to say that things are created from nothing, and in the *Short Treatise* he appeals to reason to assure us that "Something cannot come from Nothing" (I, 67). Later, in the Appendix to the exposition of Descartes, he explains that philosophers commonly write "as if nothing was the matter from which things were produced", but in so doing they fail to consider that "*nothing*" is "the negation of all reality"; instead, they "have feigned or imagined it to be something real" (I, 334). Reason, however, quickly reveals that it is a fruitless contradiction to say that something comes from nothing.

Spinoza also argues that there is no divine providence, because "if God acts for the sake of an end, he necessarily wants something that he lacks" (I, 442). This cannot be the case because God is perfect, and therefore God does not act "for the sake of an end". It follows that "all things proceed by a certain eternal necessity of nature" and "all final causes are nothing but human fictions" (I, 442).

For Spinoza, then, at the beginning there is no creation from nothing, and there are no final causes to be fulfilled at the end. Instead, the world is generated from a single, impersonal substance unfolding by necessity according to the laws of nature, to which reason gives us access. *Natura naturans* drives this process from within, along a horizontal axis from which a vertically transcendent, all-seeing, personal creator God acting freely with ends in view, is excluded. Also, for Spinoza, God is, emphatically, not personal. "What theologians understand by the term personality escapes me" (I, 206), he writes, and, again, "the term *personality*, which the Theologians commonly use" (I, 329) is useless because "we do not know its meaning, nor can we form any clear and distinct concept of it" (I, 330). Applying the idea of personality to God is merely another example of deluded anthropomorphizing, and because God cannot be said to be personal, "strictly speaking, God loves no one, and hates no one" (I, 604).

By presenting such radical criticisms of the foundations of Biblical religion, Spinoza knew that he was introducing dynamite into the glass castle of traditional Christian culture, and the inhabitants of that glass castle knew it too. But how vulnerable, in turn, was Spinoza's own reasoning? Here, it is important to recall that he was a strong foundationalist, for whom God is the guarantor of meaning. As we have seen, he held that a scientific understanding of the laws of nature gives us real knowledge of God, and the "*human Mind*" has "*an adequate knowledge of God's eternal and infinite essence*" (I, 482). But also, as a little reflection soon confirms, the chains of cause and effect in nature are so vast and intricate that we have a highly imperfect understanding of them. Moreover, because our knowledge is limited to the attributes of thought and extension, and given that God has infinite attributes, the incompleteness of our understanding is even more marked. With these points in mind, Spinoza realized that scepticism could be a tempting option, but he insisted that it was not a good one. Sceptics "say that they know nothing," he writes in the *Treatise on the Emendation of the Intellect*, "and that they do not even know that they know nothing. And even this they do not say absolutely". Consequently, such people must end up "speechless, lest by chance they assume something that might smell of truth" (I, 22). Later, he argues that "a person who does not grant himself any sound reason can not prove this by any reason" (II, 152), and he goes on to condemn the futility of those who "want to call upon reason to repudiate reason" (II, 280). Instead, Spinoza insists yet again that reason gives us access to truth and in so doing is self-authenticating and, "intelligible through itself" (I, 17). "In order for me to know, it is not necessary to know that I know" (I, 18), he argues, and "someone who has the Truth cannot doubt that he has it" (I, 120), if only because "the truth does not contradict the truth" (I, 376). He agrees that "we can doubt everything" but only "so long as we have no clear and distinct idea of God" and "the more we know natural things, the greater and more perfect is the knowledge of God we acquire" (II, 128). Reason, then, is the true religion, and Spinoza does not flinch from saying so: "man, so long as he is a part of Nature, must follow the laws of Nature. That is [true] religion" (I, 129). Once again, in secularizing the sacred, Spinoza also sacralizes the secular.

Yet Spinoza's repudiation of scepticism and his commitment to reason are also unsettled by a persistent unease having to do with a fact that the chains of cause and effect in nature are so complex as to confirm how limited our knowledge is. The intricate ways of the immanent God remain, after all, hidden from us, just as do the ways of the transcendent God of the Bible. "No one knows all the causes of things" (I, 86), Spinoza writes, "because the order of causes is hidden from us" (I, 436). Likewise, the human mind does not have "adequate knowledge of the parts composing the human body" (I, 469), and neither do we know "how each part of nature agrees with the whole" (II, 14). Simply put, nature "observes laws and rules", but "they are not all known to us" (II, 155).

Spinoza reminds us often that our knowledge is limited, and he does so partly to caution us against rushing to conclusions about miracles and the commonly held view that things are contingent. Ignorance of natural causes is a main reason why people embrace such beliefs, and yet, reason itself is frustrated by the prospect of an infinitely complex chain of causes and effects, which, ironically, can be disorienting in a manner not far removed from the endless deferral of certainty promoted by radical scepticism. In this context, Spinoza refers frequently to the notion of an infinite regress, or an infinite series, as a way of acknowledging how chains of cause and effect proliferate beyond our full comprehension. By contrast, he insists that God, the single Substance, is the uncaused origin and source of the untellable complexity, the infinite refractions within the hall of mirrors that we inhabit as we try to interpret the world. God remains the guarantor of meaning, the sole provider of stability, safeguarding us from a merely endless proliferation of fragments.

In today's secular societies, people have, by and large, abandoned Spinoza's idea of a single Substance and instead consider it normal to try to manage the endlessly reproduced, infinitely refracted supply of information that keeps us ceaselessly on the move, perpetually unstable. "Where is the wisdom we have lost in knowledge? Where is the knowledge we have lost in information?", as T.S. Eliot presciently asks,[40] anticipating a postmodern condition that has opted for its own version of Spinoza's infinite regress, an unanchored free-play of reasoning that leads at last only to an aporia amongst those who "call upon reason to repudiate reason" (II, 280). My point here is that Spinoza recognized that the power of reason to which he was so committed, despite its limitations, can also lead us into bewildering complexities. And so, in his writing, an undercurrent of anxiety runs through the very texts in which the intrepid rationalist makes his case for reason according to a "geometric method" designed to be as flawlessly convincing as it is clear. In short, Spinoza well knew that the human mind, so wonderfully capable of reason, can all too readily founder on the confusions generated by its own processes, and, in this context, his interest in the idea of an infinite regress of causes and effects appears as the shadow-side of the geometric method itself. As with Hamlet's intellectual ingenuities, an endlessly fertile pursuit of causes condemns us to a perpetual motion without resolution or certainty, unless it comes to rest on some foundation. For Spinoza, this foundation is God, the one Substance, and he worried about the consequences of its absence.

Infinite series

In Spinoza's writings, the idea of an infinite series does not pertain only to causes and effects. He saw imagination likewise as proliferating through chains of association that soon become bewildering. Also, the interpretation of texts and the resolution of controversies can remain endlessly undecided if they are disconnected from commonly accepted norms. Spinoza's awareness of these problems is registered by way of an accumulating tension in his writing between the high value he places on clarity and the confusions that arise from our "human bondage" within the labyrinth of the body. As is often pointed out, his definition of the mind as the idea of the body offers an ingenious solution to the problem of the mind-body dualism, and, as I have mentioned, he considered mind and body to be the same thing perceived by way of the attributes of thought and extension. In dispensing with dualism, this interesting theory highlights the inter-involvement between the body's felt complexities and the mind's pursuit of clarity as it seeks to understand the laws of the body's operation, which is the mind's own operation from another point of view. Clear thinking that proceeds according to the attribute of thought is therefore distinct from the body's existence considered under the attribute of extension, and yet, mind and body are the same. For human beings, thinking is not fully emancipated from the chains of cause and effect within the realm of extension, because the causes and effects always remain more intricate than thinking can grasp. Only Substance, God, can bring the perpetual motion to a safe anchorage. But, in experience, this safe anchorage is not so easily achieved – a fact that caused Spinoza some considerable unease.

The *Treatise on the Emendation of the Intellect* is a brief, unfinished enquiry about method, and in this, the earliest of his extant writings, Spinoza is already fretful about the negative consequences for philosophy of the idea of an endless series. The treatise begins with a reflection on the worldly gratifications of wealth, honour and sensual pleasure, which we are advised to avoid. Instead, we should pursue the one good that is "eternal and infinite" (I, 9), and in order to do this, "we must devise a way of healing the intellect, and purifying it" (I, 11). This emending of the intellect is what Spinoza means by "Method" which, in turn, is based on our knowing things "as directly as possible". He then pauses to reassure us "that there is no infinite regress here":

> That is, to find the best Method of seeking the truth, there is no need of another Method to seek the Method of seeking the truth, or of a third Method to seek the second, and so on, to infinity. For in that way, we would never arrive at knowledge of the truth, or indeed at any knowledge.
>
> (I, 16)

Here, Spinoza points out that the alacrity with which the mind analyses its own analyses is soon self-defeating and, as with scepticism, ends up undermining knowledge itself. We are better advised to use the tools we have, Spinoza argues, and to explain this point further, he turns again to the idea of an infinite regress. "Matters here stand as they do with corporeal tools", he writes, "where someone might argue in the same way. For to forge iron a hammer is needed; and to have a hammer, it must be made; for this another hammer, and other tools are needed; and to have these tools too, other tools will be needed, and so on to infinity; in this way someone might try, in vain, to prove that men have no power of forging iron" (I, 16). Instead of getting caught up in this kind of endless pursuit, we should get on with using the tools that are on hand. Reason is one of these, and instead of allowing reason to turn on itself in an endless series of speculative meanderings, we should use it to improve our understanding of the laws of nature and of the human condition. Although the fertility of our mental resources is admirable, Spinoza remained convinced that without foundations it is futile. The only real foundation is God, or substance, and Spinoza bases his entire epistemology on this single idea that he held to be self-evident, even though he knew it did not much appeal to "the common people". It is as if knowledge of the single substance is an ideal to which we aspire, even as we live within the gap between that ideal and an infinitely complex, material world.

In the commentary on Descartes, Spinoza is again concerned about method and about the indispensable principles that are "so clear and certain that they need no proof" (I, 231). But then, once more, the spectre of an infinite series returns to haunt the pathways along which the main arguments calmly proceed. For instance, in a departure from his main arguments about Descartes, Spinoza pauses to devote several pages to the pre-socratic philosopher, Zeno, whose "paradoxes" were aimed at denying the possibility of local motion. Spinoza cites Zeno's argument[41] (I, 270 ff.) that a single point on a revolving wheel will take a certain amount of time to return to the same place. If the wheel turns at the greatest speed possible, the time will diminish to a single moment, with the result that the point will not have moved. Spinoza responds to this argument by pointing out that we can always conceive of a faster speed, and that there is no motion without space and extension, which are always divisible into smaller units. And so, motion and time are "divisible, and this to infinity" (I, 272) and therefore Zeno's argument cannot hold. Spinoza's departure from the main commentary on Descartes, here, is significant because it shows, again, that the idea of an infinite series made a special claim on his attention. As he states in the *Appendix* to the commentary, if there were "an infinite regress" then "God would not be a most simple being, contrary to what we have demonstrated above" (I, 321).

In the *Ethics*, Spinoza returns once more to the idea of an infinite series with reference to the one Substance. He points out that we do not know the world as God does, but by way of the modes (how Substance is manifest in the material world). Also, we know one "mode again through another, and so on, to infinity" (I, 452). By contrast, God consists of "an infinity of attributes" (I, 409) which, except for the attributes of thought and extension, are unknown to us. Here, the endless interconnections amongst the modes stand over and against God's all-encompassing simplicity, which nonetheless contains a further, infinite complexity. For the present, Spinoza writes, he cannot explain these matters more clearly (I, 452), as he acknowledges a limit to his attempts to explain how the mind can be caught up in the infinite refractions of thinking, even as it holds to the certainty of the one Substance which is "by its nature, infinite, immutable, indivisible, etc., as anyone can easily see" (I, 454).

A few pages later, Spinoza returns to the idea of an endless series when he considers how "*a body which moves or is at rest must be determined to motion or rest by another, and that again by another, and so on, to infinity*" (I, 459). Individual things then are distinguished "by motion and rest, speed and slowness" (I, 461), and if we proceed "to infinity" we can "conceive that the whole of nature is one Individual" (I, 462) with an infinite variety of parts. But then, just at the point where a reader might struggle to grasp what kind of "individual" contains the infinite series without being identical with it, the authorial voice intervenes to inform us that "if it had been my intention to deal expressly with body, I ought to have explained and demonstrated these things more fully. But I have already said that I intended something else" (I, 462). Once more, the prospect of an infinite series, whether backwards or forwards, regressive or progressive, disturbs the equilibrium of the main argument and Spinoza intervenes to deflect the discussion by turning it towards "something else," more tractable. Although his foundational metaphysical principles remain in place, we feel an unease that the author is unable entirely to allay.

As we have seen, Spinoza thought that the human being is a psychophysical unity, but then he wonders, if the mind is the idea of the body does the mind also have an idea of the mind: "for as soon as someone knows something, he thereby knows that he knows it, and at the same time knows that he knows, and so on, to infinity". Having again raised the bothersome question of yet another infinite series, Spinoza deflects it by interrupting himself: "but more on these matters later" (I, 468). As in the earlier example, the deflection keeps the main argument front and centre even as a counter-current, having to do with an infinite series, unsettles it.

Later in the *Ethics*, Spinoza explains how an "*inadequate knowledge*" of the body's duration arises from the fact that duration depends on the order of nature. Its "causes" therefore are determined by other causes acting "in a certain and determinate manner, and these again by others, and so on to infinity" (I, 471). Although God has an adequate knowledge of these causes, "this knowledge is quite inadequate in our Mind" (I, 471). Spinoza then repeats the argument, stressing that "each singular thing, like the human Body, must be determined by another singular thing", "and this again by another, and so to infinity". Because of our inadequate grasp of these infinite causes, it follows that, for us, "all particular things are contingent". We have "no adequate knowledge of their duration (by P31), and that is what we must understand by the contingency of things and the possibility of their corruption" (I, 472).

This interesting reflection focuses once more on the fact that our knowledge is inadequate because the chains of cause and effect are so complex that our understanding cannot encompass them. God, the one Substance, is the sole guarantor of order, and, consequently, only in God is there "no contingency". That is, events observed from our limited point of view only appear to be contingent because we do not understand all the reasons why they could not be otherwise. And so we are to accept the demonstration that, in fact, there is no contingency, even as the weight of our lived experience causes us to think and feel differently.

The case that Spinoza makes for a universe in which everything occurs by necessity soon leads him to consider free will, and on this topic, he does not shrink from the conclusion that his ideas about contingency require: simply put, he assures us that there is no free will. Rather, "*the Mind is determined to will this or that by a cause which is also determined by another, and this again by another, and so to infinity*" (I, 483). As with contingency, our limited understanding inclines us to think that things could be otherwise (contingent), and also that we have freedom of choice. Again, the appeal to an infinite regress is a means of directing us back, however counter-intuitively, to the conviction that our confused ideas about free will are clarified only through a proper understanding of the one Substance.[42]

Spinoza's reflections on the idea of an infinite series also affect his thinking about imagination. For instance, he tells us that the will "affirms or denies something true or something false", and because the will is determined by reason "and not desire", we are to take care "that our thought does not fall into pictures" (I, 484), which only confuse and distract us from "ideas". He then insists on how important it is "to distinguish accurately between an idea, *or* concept, of the Mind and the images of things we imagine". People easily "confuse these three – ideas images, and words", and we must be careful not to "feign", or imagine, that the will is free (I, 485–6). In contrast to the confusions into which imagination leads us,

Spinoza concludes that "complete peace of mind" resides in "the knowledge of God alone" (I, 490).

Here, the suggestion that we can achieve "complete peace of mind" might strike us as itself a touch fanciful, but my main point is that, for Spinoza, imagination is volatile and endlessly deceptive. As we have seen, he was concerned to separate the idea of God from the accretions of superstition, fear mongering, and political manipulation that he found in the Bible. In the *Theological-Political Treatise* he argues that the prophets were not philosophers, but had powerful imaginations and, consequently, were all the more easily able to exert influence over the "common people" (II, 68, *et passim*) who are prone to superstition in the first place. Because of the uncertainties of human existence, people "vacillate wretchedly between hope and fear" and are "ready to believe anything whatever". They are easily "enslaved" through "the delusions of the imagination" (II, 65–6), and because the prophets had "a power of imagining unusually vividly" (II, 93), their "imagination" became identified with "the mind of God" (II, 91). As a result, the Bible frequently uses anthropomorphisms in describing God, however unacceptable these are to reason: "it's not at all surprising that the Sacred books everywhere speak so improperly about God, and attribute to him hands, feet, eyes, ears, a mind, and local motion, as well as emotions, like Jealousy, compassion, etc." (II, 62).

As an antidote to these delusions caused by imagination, Spinoza makes a distinction between religious belief and philosophy, declaring that "the main purpose" of the *Theological-Political Treatise* is "to separate faith from Philosophy" (II, 264). "There are no dealings, or no relationship, between faith, *or* Theology, and Philosophy", he argues, because "the goal of Philosophy is nothing but truth." By contrast, the goal of faith "is nothing but obedience and piety" (II, 271), and imagination is a principal means of ensuring that people remain subservient and obedient. In his earliest work, Spinoza was already concerned about these differences between truth and fiction. And so, in the *Treatise on the Emendation of the Intellect*, he insists that "no fiction is concerned with eternal truths" (I, 24). He goes on to explain that "a fictitious idea cannot be clear and distinct, but only confused", because "a fiction" is always "made from the composition of different confused ideas" (I, 29). He never departed from this line of thinking, and in the *Ethics*, he cautions readers especially about confusing ideas and images: "I begin, therefore, by warning my Readers, first, to distinguish accurately between an idea, *or* concept, of the Mind, and the images of things that we imagine" (I, 485). Because imagination is composite, it perceives "not distinctly, of course, but confusedly" (I, 547), and, as we see, he thought that this endless source of confusion could easily be manipulated by religious authorities, amongst others.

Yet Spinoza's case against imagination does not amount just to a rejection. A great deal has been written on this topic, and on how Spinoza regarded imagination as a vehicle for bringing us through the experiences of everyday life to the higher truths accessible to reason. In short, for Spinoza, imagination is ambivalent, and Eugene Garver[43] shows in detail that without imagination, Spinoza could not have written in a manner that engages us in the quest for clear reasoning in the first place. The fact is that we live in a world of finite modes where we are to some degree in bondage to our affects and passions, and here, again, a tension runs through Spinoza's writing, whereby the arguments that lead us to truth are rooted in a complex world from which reason does not entirely prise us free. Yet, my interest in Spinoza's view of imagination lies not so much in its ambivalence as in how it pertains to the idea of an infinite series. In a manner reminiscent of John Locke, he points out that imagination works largely by association, which, as with the chains of cause and effect, proliferates endlessly. Also, because interpreting the Bible stimulates a highly energetic deployment of imagination, the process spills over into the innumerable, indeed endless, factions and disputes to which religion is prone.

In a letter to Pieter Balling, Spinoza makes clear how imagination works by association. "For example, if, while we are speaking with this or that man, we hear sighs, it will generally happen that when we think again of that same man, the sighs we heard when we spoke with him will come into our memory" (I, 354). Shortly before, Spinoza had pointed out that "we can hardly understand anything of which the imagination does not form some image from a trace" (I, 353), and we have little control over such traces and how they might be connected in our mind's eye with subsequent events. Again, in the *Ethics*, when he considers the relationship between ideas and imagination, he points out that "*if the human Body has once been affected by two or more bodies at the same time, then when the Mind subsequently imagines one of them, it will immediately recollect the others also*" (I, 465). This kind of association "happens according to the order and connection of the affections", and so it is volatile. "For example, a soldier, having seen traces of a horse in the sand, will immediately pass from the thought of a horse to the thought of a horseman, and from that to the thought of war, etc. But a Farmer will pass from the thought of a horse to the thought of a plow, and then to that of a field, etc." (I, 466). Chains of association of this kind soon become too complex for us to bring fully under control, not least because "the human Mind does not know the human Body" (I, 467), and the chains of causality, fuelled by affect-based, imagined connections, are as interminable as the causes by which our bodies themselves are constituted.

Spinoza also regards contingency as a product of imagination: "it depends only on the imagination that we regard things as contingent" (I, 480). For instance, if we meet certain people regularly at appointed times during the day, we will come to associate those people with their designated meeting time. But if the schedule gets mixed up, our imagination of future meetings can easily become confused. The "imagination, therefore, will vacillate" and we "will imagine now this one, now that one". The meetings then will be "contingently future" which is to say, possible but not certain. The chains of association that enable us to imagine contingencies in this fashion stand in strong contrast to Spinoza's assurance that "it is of the nature of Reason to regard things as necessary and not as contingent" (I, 481). And so, if we understood exactly how the calendar had changed, we would not be confused about how the meeting times had changed accordingly. That is, reason will lead us beyond contingency, time, measure, and imagining.

An interesting passage in the *Theological-Political Treatise* brings together the conceptual chains of cause and effect and the imagined chains of association that I have so far been discussing. In this passage, Spinoza states that "a universal law" (II, 125) determines what happens when two bodies collide. "Similarly", he goes on, "it is a law which necessarily follows from human nature that when a man recalls one thing, he immediately recalls another like it, or one he had perceived together with the first thing" (II, 126). The first part of this statement describes causes and effects in nature; the second, chains of association by way of imagination. "Similarly" indicates that Spinoza knew how both kinds pertain to the infinite series, as he goes on to make clear. The interconnections within nature and ourselves (as part of nature) can be pursued infinitely, he writes, because "we are completely ignorant of the order and connections of things itself, i.e., of how things are really ordered and connected" (II, 126). The claim that we are "completely ignorant" is surprisingly emphatic, given that Spinoza elsewhere argues that we can have real knowledge of the laws of nature. But he then quickly pulls back to the more reserved view that we don't know how things "really" are connected. That is, our knowledge falls short of complete understanding, and yet we are not "completely" ignorant. Spinoza concludes that "for practical purposes it is better, indeed necessary" (II, 126) for us to accept that our knowledge of causes and effects is imperfect, and that we experience things as contingent, or "possible". In short, our behaviour is too complex to be governable by an appeal to metaphysical first principles alone, and in practical life we are often ambivalent, vacillating, caught up in endlessly refracting chains of reasoning and imagining that extend infinitely before and behind us. Spinoza's concept of the one Substance therefore stands in contrast to the endless confusions to which we would be condemned if we fail to acknowledge it.

As we see, Spinoza's allusions to an infinite series pertain to metaphysics (cause and effect), psychology (imagination), and in the *Theological-Political Treatise* they reach into the domain of politics and religion, as Spinoza argues for the separation of philosophy and theology because he saw how the introduction of philosophy into the exegesis of religious texts lets loose yet another infinite series of fruitless speculations to be manipulated by the authorities with a view to consolidating their power. As we have seen, he thought that the prophets had highly developed imaginations but were not philosophers: "the Prophets had only a special power to imagine things, not a special power to understand them, that God didn't reveal to them any secrets of Philosophy" (II, 257). Consequently, "the doctrine of Scripture does not contain lofty speculations, or philosophical matters" (II, 257). Rather, its central truths are "very simple" (II, 259), pertaining only to God's "Divine Justice and Loving-kindness" (II, 259). The problem with introducing "philosophic speculation" in the attempt to elucidate scripture is that the church becomes "an Academy" (II, 258), within which disputes multiply endlessly. Earlier in the *Theological-Political Treatise*, Spinoza had stressed that "everything necessary for salvation can easily be grasped" and, in the Bible, this teaching "is established only from Scripture itself" (II, 189), without the addition of philosophy. The problem with Maimonides (the medieval philosopher and Biblical commentator) is that he did not see this point clearly enough, and he thought that the Prophets "were philosophers and Theologians of the highest caliber" (II, 189). A floodgate of fruitless speculation was opened up by this assumption, proliferating endlessly because, with a little ingenuity, interpreters can take any "clearly perceived" meaning and "change it into any other meaning" (II, 190). "If it were permissible to interpret Scripture everywhere in their way, there would be absolutely no utterance whose true meaning we could not doubt"[44] (II, 235). And so, the prospect of an infinite series is, once again for Spinoza, an unsettling and threatening distraction from the plain truth.

This threatening dimension is addressed again in a discussion of Christianity and the state, in which Spinoza explains how the Ecclesiastical authorities "increased the doctrines of Religion" and in so doing "confused them so much with Philosophy that the supreme interpreter of Religion had to be a supreme Philosopher or Theologian". One result was the production of "a great many useless speculations: (II, 342) that were developed to buttress the mystique of the Ecclesiastics against the power of "Christian Kings". In turn, during the Reformation, this same proliferation of theories is "the principal reason why the sectaries teach as doctrines of the faith so many and such contrary opinions" (II, 264). Sectarianism and its fractious, often violent consequences are therefore fuelled by an interminable theorizing, endlessly reproduced. Such disputes "could never be settled. For where men begin to argue with the fierce heat of superstition, and the magistrate aids one or the other side, they can never be calmed" (II, 325). In the turmoil of this kind of divisiveness and disputation, the plain truth is easily forgotten, namely, that no one really "acknowledges God, except by Loving-kindness toward his neighbour" (II, 267). Neither the distractions of imagination nor the conceptual ingenuities of philosophy should obscure this universal principle. With this in mind, and to curtail as many further confusions and divisions as possible, Spinoza declares that "the main purpose" of the *Theological-Political Treatise* is "to separate faith from Philosophy" (II, 264).

Self-interest and seeking truth with others

It is helpful now briefly to reconsider the point of tension in Spinoza's work that I described earlier, between an egoistic approach to ethics and a contrary impulse to transcend egoism in the interests of loving one's neighbour and promoting the common good. Steven Nadler points out that egoism is at "the heart" of Spinoza's "system"[45], but that Spinoza also recommends "benevolent and considerate ways of treating other human beings" (238): "enlightened egoism, in other words, leads to maximal mutual utility" (242). Nadler adds that "Spinoza's claims are of course highly paradoxical" (242), and I want to attend a little further the relationship between "paradoxical" and "enlightened", with a view to considering how, for Spinoza, mere individualism produces a further, endless series that undermines the common good as well as commonly shared understandings.

Certainly, Spinoza is unequivocal in declaring the connection between self-interest and ethical behaviour when he writes in the *Ethics* that "the striving to preserve oneself is the first and only foundation of virtue." He emphasizes that "acting absolutely from virtue is nothing but acting from the laws of our own nature", which is to say "from the foundation of seeking one's own advantage" (I, 558). The same point is made in the *Political Treatise*: "both in the natural state and in the civil order, man acts according to the laws of his own nature and looks out for his own advantage". Within the civil order, that is, everyone who obeys the laws is in fact "surely looking out for his own security and his own advantage." (II, 518).

Yet, Spinoza also held that self-interest is served by benevolence: "he who lives according to the guidance of reason, desires for the other, too, the good he wants for himself" (I, 575). Here, it is clear, as Steven Nadler says, that "enlightened egoism" can promote "enlightened utility", and it is a fundamental tenet of social contract theory that our own interests are served when our relations with others are mutually beneficial. But the full picture, for Spinoza, is more complicated. In the *Short Treatise on the Emendation of the Intellect*, he assures us that "we need no principle other than that of seeking our own advantage" (I, 146–7), but then, a few pages later, he advises that we "should have no other aim or motive than the salvation of your fellow man" (I, 150). This second injunction registers a significant shift from the position stated in the first, because the words, "no other aim or motive" advise us to transcend self-interest as our primary incentive. The salvation of others, here, is the main concern. It could be argued that the context requires us to understand that in sharing with others we provide a benefit to them that we already enjoy, and so there is no sacrifice of self-interest. But the words, "no other aim or motive" are clear, and here, as elsewhere, Spinoza declares an uneasiness about egoism being a sufficient motive for virtuous action. And so, in the *Short Treatise on the Emendation of the Intellect*, Love states that "my being and perfection depend entirely on your perfection" (I, 73), and in a letter to Pieter Balling, Spinoza offers the bereaved father an assurance that "a father so loves his son that he and his beloved son are, as it were, one and the same" (I, 353). In these examples, the boundaries between self and other are porous, and the good of the other is also one's own good, realized through a participatory exchange in which the ego does not simply stand over and against others, but is in part already constituted by them. As I have mentioned, Étienne Balibar uses the term "transindividual" to describe this dynamic interdependence between self and other, and although I prefer the word "personal", the underlying point is the same. Spinoza's intimations of and aspirations to a fulfilment beyond mere individualism are central to his thinking, and the prospect of innumerable individuals competing endlessly for their own satisfaction is incoherent and unsustainable. As with metaphysics, imagination, and interpretation, an interminable replication needs to come to rest on some higher governing principle or value.

And so, in *God, Man and his Well-Being*, Spinoza argues that the highest knowledge (what he would later call intuition) "produces love; so if we come to know God in this way, then we must necessarily unite with him" (I, 139). Earlier, in the *Treatise on the Emendation of the Intellect*, he had argued along the same lines that "the highest good" is "the knowledge of the union that the mind has with the whole of Nature", and that we should "arrive" at this good together with others, "if possible". In turn, this union of minds is the foundation of a good society (I, 10–11). And so, Love of God is our own highest good as well as the good of others in society, even though, in the imperfect world in which we live, we often look out for our own interests first. In the *Theological-Political Treatise*, Spinoza again makes clear that the happiness "of each person" does not consist in "a self-esteem founded on the fact that he alone enjoys the good", and "whoever views himself as more blessed because things are well with him, but not with others … does not know true happiness". To think otherwise is "mere childishness" (II, 111). Here, Spinoza confirms that merely self-interested gratification falls short of "true happiness", and the exclusion of others from one's own well-being is childish – which is to say, a phase that we need to pass beyond. In turn, this passage leads us back to the *Short Treatise on God, Man and his Well-Being*, where Spinoza uses language uncharacteristically close to the Christian idea of being born again:

> For our first birth was when we were united with the body. From this union have arisen the effects and motions of the [animal] spirits. But our other, or second, birth will occur when we become aware in ourselves of the completely different effects of love produced by knowledge of this incorporeal object. This [love of God] is as different from [love of the body] as the incorporeal is from the corporeal, the spirit from the flesh.
>
> This, therefore may the more rightly and truly be called Rebirth, because, as we shall show, an eternal and immutable constancy comes only from this Love and Union.
>
> (I, 140)

Read in isolation, this passage would be difficult to identify as Spinoza's, but we need to remind ourselves that the "second birth" here is not a gift of divine grace, as in Christianity, but an awakening of the mind to the one substance that we can know by exercising our reason, and as a result of which we experience joy. In the *Ethics*, Spinoza explains that knowledge increases our power, and joy then arises naturally. Because our highest knowledge is the "intellectual Love of God", the joy that accompanies it is "eternal" (I, 611), and this is also what Spinoza means by rebirth in the *Short Treatise on the Emendation of the Intellect*. In both texts, he calls upon his readers to abandon a life lived in bondage to the passions, the endless confusions of imagination, the tyranny of superstition and interminable sectarian feuds. Rebirth does not occur through supernatural intervention, but by an exercise of our natural capabilities, and in the shaping of "a pact of friendship with people who sincerely love the truth" (I, 357). And so, the idea of a spiritual rebirth pertains especially to groups of philosophical seekers bound together by the fact that "the love they bear to one another is based on the love each has for knowledge of the truth" (I, 357).

In his helpful article on friendship in Spinoza, Frank Lukash[46] considers the self-interest theory in detail and poses the question of whether or not Spinoza would approve of the idea of giving one's life for one's friend. Lukash concludes that "my reading of Spinoza would probably indicate a negative answer". Yet, "probably" is well chosen because we can't be sure, and, as is often the case, Spinoza's main arguments are disturbed by the counter-currents that they themselves generate. Just as he suggests that there are limits to self-centredness, so we might expect to discover that there are limits also to altruism. Spinoza does not deal systematically with this set of issues, however, and he might well have realized that people's attitudes would vary according to the gradations of awareness that he describes. First, as we see, is the "childish" phase in which we are prone to delusion and driven by selfishness. This stage then yields to an attitude of enlightened self-interest, a hard-headed assessment of mutual benefit as, for instance, in the busy world of the market and the lawcourts. A third level comprises lovers or truth for its own sake, the band of friends whose interests touch upon and are touched by eternity, and who are united in the love of truth through that aspect of their minds that Spinoza describes as eternal (I, 614).

Complexities and tensions run through these gradations or stages, as is also the case more generally with Spinoza's work. As I have attempted to show, his carefully reasoned arguments are everywhere disturbed by the felt pressure of an often not explicitly declared counter case. He well knew that the struggle for truth is arduous and people often work against their own interests, keen to "fight for slavery as they would for their survival" (II, 68). In every age, human beings have "always been the same", but "in every age virtue has been extremely rare" (II, 249), not least because reason has a tenuous hold on our emotions. We "love or hate some things without any cause known to us" (I, 503), the mind "*does not have an absolute dominion*" (I, 595), and "experience teaches all too well that it's no more in our power to have a sound Mind than it is to have a sound Body" (II, 509). Expecting "most people" to be able "to live wisely" is therefore "impossible", and this being the case, people should be "guided by affects more advantageous to the Republic" (II, 599) and act according to prudent self-interest. But what, then, about the minority joined in the "pact of friendship of those who love the truth?" (I, 357). Spinoza himself experienced this kind of friendship when he associated with assorted free-thinkers and others who, in a spirit of free enquiry, challenged the prevailing orthodoxies and often suffered for their opinions, sometimes in an extreme way, as in the case of Spinoza's friend Adriaan Koerbach.[47] Spinoza never lost touch with his Amsterdam friends, and in a letter to Willem van Blijenburgh, he describes "the honor of entering into a pact of friendship with people who sincerely love the truth", adding that "we can love none tranquilly, except such people. Because the love they bear to one another is based on the love each has for knowledge of the truth" (I, 357). In the *Ethics* he confirms this opinion by explaining that "only free men" are "joined to one another by the greatest necessity of friendship" (I, 586), and if we live "according to the guidance of reason" and seek the good, we will "strive to have others love the same thing" so that the goal is "common to all" (I, 565). In short, the search for truth by a minority of like-minded seekers is a main means of finding a way forward towards real understanding in a world otherwise beset by endless individual self-assertion, superstition, faction and confusion.

Conclusion

In his exegesis of a selection of Biblical references to "spirit" and "heart", Spinoza clarifies what is required for the co-operative search for truth that he most admired. The epigraph in the *Theological-Political Treatise* cites I John 4:13: "By this we know that we remain in God and that God remains in us, because he has given us of his Spirit" (II, 65). Spinoza explains that there are several meanings of "spirit" in the Hebrew Bible – for instance, referring to God's "kindness and compassion" as "affects of the heart" (II, 90). In addition, "the Hebrews believed the heart to be the seat of the soul and of the intellect" (II, 117). Saint Paul teaches that faith requires "a full consent of the heart" (II, 134), and Spinoza argues that in the Bible, "the better we know someone's spirit and mentality, the more easily we can explain his words" (II, 175). The Apostles teach that the covenant is not now written "with ink", but "on the heart, by the Spirit of God" (II, 322), and whoever has "salutary opinions and a true manner of living … really has the Spirit of Christ in him" (II, 150).

These references to "spirit" and "heart" are not systematic and are loosely applied to fit the context. Yet, broadly, "spirit" indicates, for Spinoza, a quality of engagement – a "mentality" and a "manner of living", as well as "affects of the heart". The values associated with these words sustain the groups of friends who are searching for the truth beyond self-interest. Balibar describes this process as "transindividual", and, along the same lines, I have suggested that it is "personal" and I would also want to claim that the spirit and "manner" in which this kind of discourse is conducted is dialogical. As Spinoza well knew, the work of dialogue is unfinished in a world where it is "impossible", as he says, for most people to act wisely. But the discussion of ideas in a spirit of non-egoistical love for the truth can nonetheless help us to glimpse what a good society might be. As he wrote in the *Treatise on God, Man and his Well-Being*, "our perfection … consists in this, that we must always strive to attain more and more" (I, 128). Reason, intellect and intuition promise to bring us certainty, joy and freedom, but Spinoza's arguments in favour of these values also bear the marks of a striving that results from our limited capacities and the imperfections of human society. Reason remains our best guide, but reason also shows us why it is difficult for reason to prevail, and Spinoza's writing is shot through with indications of concern about the uncertain purchase his arguments might have on the everyday world. I have suggested that the several undercurrents of concern in his work can be seen and felt especially in his interest in, even preoccupation with, the idea of an infinite series. Endless chains of cause and effect, the unconstrained play of imagination, interminable processes of free association and endless interpretations opening on yet further unresolvable disputes haunt Spinoza's arguments about reason, truth and stable meaning like a bad dream. As a confident Modernity unfolded during the following centuries towards the cultural crisis of Modernism, Spinoza's concerns about a culture without stable foundations or an over-arching vision would become much more than merely an undercurrent.

Notes

1 The ways in which both the Reformation and the New Science emphasized God's ineffable transcendence, thus preparing the way for secularism, is explored in Patrick Grant, *Literature and the Discovery of Method in English Renaissance* (London: Macmillan, 1985).

2 As Karl Jaspers points out in *Spinoza*, ed. Hannah Arendt, trans. Ralph Manheim (New York: Harcourt Brace Jovanovich, 1966; first published, 1957), p. 9: "This total vision came to Spinoza suddenly, almost complete from the first moment". Jonathan I. Israel adds that in the late 1650s, Spinoza's discovery of Cartesian philosophy was "decisive and formative", and it also intensified his earlier enquires. See Jonathan I. Israel, *Spinoza, Life and Legacy* (Oxford: Oxford University Press, 2023), p. 327.

3 See Steven Nadler, *Spinoza. A Life* (Cambridge: Cambridge University Press, 1999), pp. 42 ff., for a further account of Spinoza's name.

4 See Nadler, *Spinoza. A Life*, p. 63, and Israel, *Spinoza, Life and Legacy*, p. 171, on Spinoza's knowledge of "Torah and Hebrew reaching a fairly sophisticated level".

5 See Israel, *Spinoza, Life and Legacy*, p. 273: "All Spinoza scholars agree the evidence points to Spinoza experiencing encounters with Amsterdam's religious fringe groups, especially Collegiants, from even before his separation from the Jewish community".

6 Israel, *Spinoza, Life and Legacy*, p. 261.

7 See Israel, *Spinoza, Life and Legacy*, pp. 229 ff.

8 See Nadler, *Spinoza. A Life*, pp. 66 ff, 130 ff.

9 A lawsuit, by means of which Spinoza avoided assuming his father's debts while also renouncing his inheritance was conducted outside the Jewish community, and it would have confirmed to the community that Spinoza was a serious troublemaker. See Israel's *Spinoza, Life and Legacy*, p. 222 ff.

10 These words are attributed to Spinoza by his early biographer, Jean-Maximilian Lucas, cited in Nadler, *Spinoza. A Life*, p. 154.

11 See Edwin Curley, *The Collected Works of Spinoza*, 2 vols. (New Jersey: Princeton University Press, 1985, 2016), I, 3, citing Letter 6. All further references are cited in the text.

12 Curley, *Collected Works*, I, 51.

13 Curley, *Collected Works*, I, 405.

14 For an account of Spinoza as "supreme philosophical bogeyman", see Jonathan I. Israel, *Radical Enlightenment. Philosophy and the Making of Modernity 1650-1750* (Oxford: Oxford University Press, 2001), pp. 151 ff; on the widespread vilification of Spinoza, see pp. 161 ff; on reactions against the *Theological-Political Treatise*, see pp. 275 ff.

15 Henri Bergson, *La Pensée et le mouvant: essais en conférences*, 5th ed. (Paris: Alcan, 1934), p. 142, cited in Steven Nadler, *Spinoza's Ethics* (Cambridge: Cambridge University Press, 2006), p. 35.

16 Antonio Negri, *The Savage Anomaly: The Power of Spinoza's Metaphysics and Politics*, trans. Michael Hardt (Minnesota: University of Minnesota Press, 1991), p. 48; Jaspers, *Spinoza*, pp. 24, 32; Gilles Deleuze, *Spinoza. Practical Philosophy*, trans. Robert Hurley (San Francisco: City Lights Books, 1988; first published, 1970), pp. 14, 129. Matthew Stewart, *The Courtier and the Heretic. Leibniz, Spinoza, and the Fate of God in the Modern World* (New York: W. W. Norton and Co., 2006), p. 163, draws attention to the "aesthetic experience" of reading the *Ethics*, which is "in some ways like a prose poem". Clare Carlisle, *Spinoza's Religion. A New Reading of the Ethics* (Princeton: Princeton University Press, 2021), p. 11, describes the *Ethics* as "a literary work of art".

17 In the *Ethics*, Spinoza makes the bold proposal that "*The human mind has an adequate knowledge of God's eternal and infinite essence*" (I. 482).

18 On final causes, see, for example, *Ethics*, I, 440–1, and on miracles, I, 443. These positions are further developed in the *Ethics* and in the *Theological-Political Treatise*.

19 On God's freedom, see *Ethics*, I, 425.

20 See *Ethics*, I, 544.

21 On the eternal element of the mind, see *Ethics*, I, 607, 614–5.

22 See Israel, *Radical Enlightenment*, p. 259: "Effectively, Spinoza was the first major European thinker in modern times – though he is preceded here by Johan de la Court and Van den Enden – to embrace democratic republicanism as the highest and most fully rational form of political organization, and the one best suited to the needs of men".

23 Thomas Carlyle, *Sartor Resartus*, ed. Kerry McSweeney and Peter Sabor (Oxford: Oxford University Press, 2008; first published, 1987), pp. 193 ff. See also M. H. Abrams, *Natural Supernaturalism, Tradition and Revolution in Romantic Literature* (New York: W. W. Norton and Co., 1971), for an account of the broad implications of the new perspective.

24 See Clare Carlisle and Yitzhak Y. Malamed, "God-Intoxicated Men", *The Times Literary Supplement*, 15 May, 2020.
25 As is often pointed out, the term "atheism" was loosely used in Spinoza's time, and often it is not clear what the accusations mean.
26 See, for instance, Helena Petrovna Blavatsky, *Madame Blavatsky on Spinoza and Western Philosophers*, Blavatsky Speaks Series, contributor, Carl Onion (UK: Philalethians, 2018). The essay was originally published in *The Theosophist* LXXXIII, no. 7 (April, 1962): 6–13.
27 Charles Taylor, *A Secular Age* (Cambridge, MA: Harvard University Press, 2007), p. 535.
28 Roger Scruton, *Spinoza. A Very Short Introduction* (Oxford: Oxford University Press, 2002; first published, 1986), p. 41, points out that Spinoza's "axioms are far from self-evident, and derive their claim to be 'adequate' only in the course of proofs which already assume them to be so".
29 Nadler, *Spinoza's Ethics. An Introduction*, pp. 47–8.
30 Jaspers, *Spinoza*, p. 23. Jaspers also adds that Spinoza regarded his arguments as wholly persuasive and without contradiction.
31 Friedrich Nietzsche, *Beyond Good and Evil*, I, 6, trans. Marianne Cowan (Chicago: Henry Regnery, 1966), p. 6.
32 See Christopher Norris, *Spinoza and the Origins of Modern Critical Theory* (Oxford: Basil Blackwell, 1991), Introduction by Michael Payne, p. 3.
33 Deleuze, *Spinoza. Practical Philosophy*, p. 26.
34 Deleuze, *Spinoza. Practical Philosophy*, p. 122.
35 Mattew Stewart, *The Courtier and the Heretic*, p. 104; Étienne Balibar, *Spinoza the Transindividual*, trans. Mark G. E. Kelly (Edinburgh: Edinburgh University Press, 2020).
36 Deleuze, *Spinoza. Practical Philosophy*, p. 130.
37 Carlisle, *Spinoza's Religion*, p. 66.
38 This is argued by Leo Strauss, *Persecution and the Art of Writing* (Chicago: University of Chicago Press, 1988; first published, 1952), and, with various modifications, by others. For an assessment of this position, see Curley, *Complete Works*, I, 53.
39 Edwin Curley's conclusion, cited earlier, that "there is no easy way to label his [Spinoza's] position" is confirmed by Clare Carlisle, *Spinoza's Religion*, p. 7.
40 T. S. Eliot, *Choruses from 'The Rock'*, I, in *Selected Poems* (London: Faber and Faber, 1961), p. 107.
41 As Curley points out, this argument "is not to be found in any of our ancient sources of knowledge of Zeno" (I, 270). Curley also notes that Spinoza's reflections on Zeno "go well beyond Descartes' sketchy reflections on those topics" (I, 222). In so doing, they highlight Spinoza's special concerns.
42 The conundrum is put succinctly by Samuel Johnson: "All theory is against the freedom of the will; all experience for it". See James Boswell, *Life of Samuel Johnson* (New York: Everyman's Library, 1906), p. 833.
43 Eugene Garver, *Spinoza and the Cunning of Imagination* (Chicago: University of Chicago Press, 2018).
44 Christopher Norris, *Spinoza and the Origins of Modern Critical Theory*, makes the case that Spinoza's biblical criticism lays the groundwork for modern critical and theoretical approaches to literature.
45 Nadler, *Spinoza's Ethics*, pp. 238, 242.
46 Frank Lukash, "Spinoza on Friendship", *Philosophia* 40 (2012): 305–17.
47 See Israel, *Spinoza, Life and Legacy*, pp. 599 ff; Nadler, *Spinoza. A Life*, pp. 265 ff.

3 Interlude

From Modernity to Modernism

As Jonathan Israel[1] points out, "Spinozism" in the seventeenth and eighteenth centuries was not so much a set of arguments as a new, broadly challenging view of the world – a set of attitudes as well as a set of propositions. I have suggested that Spinoza's thinking was integral to the shaping of Modernity, but also that he was aware of a shadow side to his own main arguments. That is, if reason were not grounded in metaphysical first principles, and if nature were to become disconnected from the philosophical God that reason shows us exists, we would be left with a bad infinity of aimless processes in nature and in human thinking – processes devoid of foundations and, therefore, devoid of enduring and dependable meaning. And so, I have suggested that the cool surfaces of Spinoza's arguments are agitated by an underlying concern about something very like the *anomie* later described by Durkheim as a "malady of the infinite".[2]

In dispensing with the traditional Biblical creator God, Spinoza blurred the boundary between sacred and secular, but his reasons for going on then to identify God and Substance are a great deal less compelling today than his appropriation of the divine agency to a view of nature as a rule-governed, dynamic process. In 1859, Darwin's *On the Origin of Species* described evolution as a purposeless mechanism of selection and survival, and in that light it was especially unconvincing to suggest that the human condition cannot be properly understood without the metaphysical foundations on which Spinoza insisted. The hard truth seemed unavoidable: we are alone in nature which operates cruelly and without purpose. Today, alienation, absurdity and *anomie* have become familiar currency for describing this situation.

Nonetheless, in his own time, Spinoza's arguments did not prevent most people from continuing to believe in the Biblical God, but in the eighteenth century, the Enlightenment, relieved of the burden of medieval metaphysics and buoyed up by the success and growing prestige of science, offered a powerful critique of the moral imperfections of much that passed for religion and Voltaire's *écrasez l'infame* rang out to the discomfiture of a great many orthodox believers. When Enlightenment reason and science combined then with *laissez-faire* economics to fuel a rapidly progressing industrialization, the

DOI: 10.4324/9781003546856-3

resultant, damaging effects were countered by Romantic appeals to nature as a healing, restorative agency that re-connects us with the deep, life-affirming sources of ourselves. The great Victorians, including Van Gogh's favourites, Thomas Carlyle and George Eliot, were shaped by the challenges presented by these interconnected developments. As unbelievers, they nonetheless acknowledged the moral insights and continuing cultural influence of Christianity as they attempted also to formulate a view of the world that was at once secular, moral and responsive to the deep embeddedness of human beings in nature and which resisted the alienations caused by industrialization.

By and large, in the later nineteenth century, mainstream social attitudes continued to draw on a rich but complex tradition of values and ideas variously combined and re-combined to sustain a general confidence in science, the idea of progress, the market economy, capitalism and conservative civilized norms. And yet, all too clearly, *laissez-faire* economics and industrialization were causing the kinds of grave, widespread immiseration that called forth Marx's critique of the entire capitalist system. Towards the end of the nineteenth century, Durkheim coined the term *anomie*, or "normlessness", to describe the profound alienations following upon the dehumanizing conditions that had become all too disturbingly prevalent. For Durkheim, as for Marx, mass industrialization broke the connection between workers and what they produced, and also between workers and traditional communities. Consequently, people in industrialized societies found themselves undermined by an alienation and rootlessness that corroded their sense of identity and purpose. Under such conditions, Durkheim argued, desire is cut loose from realistic, communally supported expectations, spilling over instead into resentful and destructive behaviour – including suicide. At the end of the nineteenth century, the crisis represented by *anomie* had become especially urgent because on so many fronts the traditional underpinnings of the social order were buckling under the weight of the criticisms imposed on them. The effort of regathering what was left of those underpinnings with a view to making something new is, in a nutshell, what is meant by Modernism, and Ezra Pound's declaration in 1934, "Make it New"[3] is often taken to represent a main impulse of the new movement. Yet, Pound was anticipated by Van Gogh,[4] who likewise declared his desire to "make all things new" (101/1, 138; 120/1, 175) and to present the fragmented world around him "in a new light" (152/1, 242).

From his earliest years, Van Gogh was an outsider, an oddball who didn't fit in. His sister, Lies, described his strange solitude, and how different he was from his siblings.[5] He had difficulty holding a job, and was fired by his first employer, Goupil & Cie., in The Hague, where he began working when he was 16. His subsequent attempts at regular employment in a stationery store (kantoorboekhandel) in Dordrecht and as a lay evangelist amongst the Borinage miners in Belgium ended in failure and disappointment. He had sought refuge in religion, but he came to see the traditional, bourgeois Christianity of his parents as a betrayal of what Jesus really meant, especially with regard to caring for the poor and the dispossessed. The plight of the Borinage miners revealed all too clearly the depredations of industrialization and elicited from Van Gogh a fierce moral protest that also fuelled his critique of conventional Christian observance. When, in The Hague, he took up with the pregnant, ex-part-time prostitute, Sien Hoornik, he encountered a ferocious reaction from his family, confirming his alienation from the middle-class values they had raised him to observe. Both before and after Sien, his attempts to make close personal relationships with women failed miserably and sadly. His recently widowed and grieving cousin, Kee, turned his advances down flat, and his subsequent attempt to live with the damaged and dysfunctional Sien was undermined by her family as well as his, and also by the fact that he and Sien were all but impossible to live with anyway. In Nuenen, where he then moved, the unfortunate Margot Begemann ended her apparently amorous relationship with him by attempting suicide, and when his father died soon afterwards, his family turned angrily against him. Already, when Vincent was in the Borinage, his father had concerns about his son's mental health and took steps to have him committed. The sense that there was something crazy about Vincent persisted throughout his life, and eventually, he sought refuge in an asylum for the mentally ill, following the famous self-mutilation when he sliced off a piece of his left ear. Not long after, even as his painting began to attract serious recognition, he died by his own hand at age 37.

In Chapter 4, I will return in more detail to Van Gogh's biography. For now, I want only to indicate the extent of his alienation from the conventional middle-class world in which he grew up, and how this alienation began in earnest with the discovery that traditional Christianity could not meet the challenges posed by human suffering and immiseration, especially the kind caused by industrialization. His parents' traditional Christian values also failed to meet the test of his unconventional love relationships, and Vincent furiously denounced their opinions as illiberal and cruel. And so, increasingly for Van Gogh the centre did not hold, and his art alone provided him with bearings, even as his paintings were consistently rejected and even ridiculed.

As his career drew to a premature close and the value of his art began to be recognized, Van Gogh, paradoxically, was becoming increasingly aware of the insufficiency of painting to satisfy his aspirations to a fulfilled life. His experiences of alienation, rootlessness and exile (many of the great Modernists were exiles) gave rise then to an intense, diffuse longing for the infinite, not the rootless malaise described by Durkheim, but the promise of a new kind of aspiration and spiritual awareness that could be the foundation of a good human community. In light of his death by suicide, *anomie* might seem to have won the day, and yet, Van Gogh's paintings, increasingly symbolic and self-referential (or figural, as I will argue), were reaching towards the further vision that he felt would subsume art and be the antidote to the worst that a lifetime of suffering and loneliness could effect. For its part, art would maintain its integrity by resisting commodification and any mere catering to fashion. To avoid these pitfalls, an artist might have to resort to discontinuities, indirections and self-reflexivity, so that the viewer or reader's attention is turned towards the internal processes of the work, in contrast to the more self-assured, accessible conventions of realistic representation. As with Van Gogh's paintings, Modernist art in general is difficult to access, a strategy deployed by artists to suggest that value has to be sought out, discovered and constructed rather than authoritatively imparted and passively received. The Modernists who staked a great deal on symbolic indirection and discontinuity hovering on the edge of incoherence did so on the conviction that values could still be affirmed, even if it is difficult to define or name them.

One reason why Van Gogh's letters are compelling is that they are so thoroughly Modernist, both in content and composition. The discontinuous narrative they present is a sort of fragmentary *bildungsroman*, replete with conflicts, disconcerting indirections and challenges to the reader (whether the actual recipients or ourselves). And yet, the correspondence as a whole has an underlying integrity, an imaginative coherence driven by a relentless search for meaning and value in the chaotic world that drove Van Gogh to seek new ways of communicating, both in his paintings and drawings, as well as in his writing.[6] The circumstances that gave rise to the chaos and *anomie* he experienced throughout his life are described with special clarity in the series of letters written to Émile Bernard in 1888. Van Gogh points out that artists in the Middle Ages and Renaissance lived in an "architecturally constructed" society, whereas today "we're in a state of total laxity and anarchy" (655/4, 216). The artist has now become an isolated figure, "exiled, a social outcast". Whores (for whom Van Gogh had a great deal of sympathy) are "like you and I surely are, 'outcasts' too", in contrast to "those who pimp for a living" along with their "well-fed clients" (655/4, 218). The comparison here between whores and artists refers to the fact that artists were forced to sell themselves in the new entrepreneurial art trade recently developed in Paris as a reaction against the state-sponsored Salon system. Galleries, dealers and critics counted on a newly capitalized art market to develop a competitive business for the buying and selling of paintings.[7] The first beneficiaries were the Impressionists, the *refusés* whose work had been rejected by the Salon and who, consequently, sought further outlets in an attempt to make a living. Vincent's brother Theo was highly successful in this new world of art dealing, even as, paradoxically, the artists themselves – Vincent amongst them – were doing what they could to resist having their work seen merely as another commodity.[8] This complex state of affairs is represented in a persistent, unresolved conflict in Van Gogh's letters between his frequently stated contempt for art dealers and his desire for dealers to sell his work so that he could make a living. On occasion, as we will see in Chapter 4, he berated Theo bitterly for not doing enough to develop a market for his paintings, even as he angrily deplored the easy gratifications of consumerism and the bad taste of art dealers, as well as a gullible public. Admittedly, Van Gogh's preoccupation with making his work saleable reflects his unease at being dependent on Theo's generous monthly stipend, but the dilemma ran deeper, and it dogged Vincent to the very end. It is not unlikely that his guilt about imposing an intolerable financial burden on his recently married brother, who now also had a baby son, contributed to Vincent taking his own life. As he explained to Bernard, "society makes our existence wretchedly difficult at times, hence our impotence and the imperfection of our work" (III, 525). For Van Gogh, that is, the artist remained an *isolé*, caught up in a fraught search for meaning and value that in earlier civilizational phases were more directly imparted, and which now have to be made new in a world so imperfect that the very attempt at making new is itself compromised by the mechanisms through which the results are promoted. The *aporia*, which is to say, the sense of impotency within a prevailing "anarchy", as Van Gogh describes it, is itself the nameless place from which he thought a new religion as yet with "no name" would emerge, and the authentic way forward lay for him, as it still does, through the *aporia* itself. Everywhere, he compels us to feel the weight of this challenge, which his art reveals as a living witness to his own struggle. In a different mode, this struggle is also described in his jagged, often conflicted, but compelling correspondence which, I will want to claim, charts the main crises in the development itself of Modernism from Modernity by way of Van Gogh's own personal journey. Today, no secular culture can avoid encountering, in one form or another, the challenges posed by that cultural evolution and its postmodern aftermath.

In pointing us towards an as yet nameless religion of the future, Van Gogh anticipated a situation today in which the main established religious traditions can no longer credibly claim to possess the one saving truth to the exclusion of all the others. Rather, a sense of some broader, more encompassing search or synthesis in the making is pervasive in the cultural phase in which we live, and in this context, as Van Gogh shows us, art opens upon a mystery, inviting us to consider it as a source of creativity and communion. Today, the highly developed conceptual apparatus and symbolic repertoire of the main religious traditions might help to stabilize people's encounter with this invitation, placing it within a coherent cultural narrative, recapitulating all that we have been from our deepest origins to the furthest reaches of the most adequate stories that we tell ourselves. We might then be better able to avoid the distortions that occur when the full range of our evolved capacities is not acknowledged and deployed in our everyday lives. As Van Gogh reminds us, a critical encounter with the cultural resources that have made us what we are is necessary if the best of what those resources offer is to take us beyond their limitations, to the point at which the sources themselves are transfigured and made new.

Notes

1 Jonathan I. Israel, *Radical Enlightenment. Philosophy and the Making of Modernity (1650-1750)* (Oxford: Oxford University Press, 2001).
2 See Chapter 1, note 20.
3 Ezra Pound, *Make It New. Essays by Ezra Pound* (London: Faber and Faber, 1934).
4 *Vincent van Gogh: The Letters*, ed. Leo Jansen, Hans Luijten, and Nienke Bakker, 6 vols. (New York and London: Thames and Hudson, 2009). Letter numbers are cited in the text, with the volume and page number following the forward slash. An expanded version on which the printed edition is based is available free of charge at www.vangoghletters.org.
5 Elizabeth du Quesne-Van Gogh, "Vincent Van Gogh" (1910), in Susan Alyson Stein, ed. *Van Gogh. A Retrospective* (New York: Park Lane, 1986), pp. 31–2.
6 The letters have been slow to receive the critical attention they deserve. See Patrick Grant, *The Letters of Vincent van Gogh. A Critical Study* (Edmonton: Athabasca University Press, 2014); *My Own Portrait in Writing. Self-Fashioning in the Letters of Vincent van Gogh* (Edmonton: Athabasca University Press, 2015); *Reading Vincent van Gogh. A Thematic Guide to the Letters* (Edmonton: Athabasca University Press, 2016).
7 See Steven Naifeh and Gregory White Smith, *Van Gogh. The Life* (New York: Random House, 2011), pp. 543 ff.; Cornelia Homburg, "Vincent van Gogh and the Avant-Garde: Colleagues, Competitors, Friends", in *Vincent's Choice. The Musée Imaginaire of Van Gogh*, ed. Chris Stolwijk, Sjraar van Heugten, Leo Jansen and Adreas Blühm (Van Gogh Museum: Amsterdam, 2003), pp. 199 ff.
8 This is persuasively argued by Terry Eagleton, *Against the Grain: Essays 1975-1985* (London: Verso, 1986), pp. 140 ff.

4 Van Gogh and Modernism

Recapitulation and making new

Like Spinoza, Vincent van Gogh is a singular figure whose work represents in a highly illuminating way the main forces at work in the shaping of the civilizational phase in which it was produced. In the following pages, I want to suggest that one aspect of Van Gogh's cultural significance is that his life and work recapitulate the process itself of the emergence of Modernism from the blueprint of Modernity laid down by Spinoza. That is, as an evangelist, a moral reformer and a lover of nature who went on to explore the possibilities and limits of the aesthetic, Van Gogh mirrors the cultural trajectory leading from the Reformation to the Enlightenment, Romanticism and the self-reflexive Modernist experiments that were taking shape, especially in Paris, at the end of the nineteenth century.

Throughout his career, Van Gogh wrestled with the elusive interconnections amongst religion, morality and art, and he did not abandon any one of these topics entirely as another became the main focus of his attention.[1] For example, in his early religious phase, morality and art were ancillary to his evangelism. Later, when he rejected orthodox Christianity and became preoccupied with the plight of the poor, he insisted that his new commitment reflected the true spirit of Christianity, with which too many orthodox Christians had lost touch, and he planned to publish in illustrated magazines in order to draw attention to the social evils that caused him so much concern. Art therefore would be deployed in the service of morality, informed by what Van Gogh took to be a true Christian spirit.

When his aspirations to become an illustrator did not work out, Van Gogh became preoccupied with the idea that colour could communicate independently of the narrative dimension required by his socially engaged illustrations. Colour is a powerful means for revealing the deepest bonds between human beings and nature, and so, when his morally earnest, Enlightenment critique had exhausted itself, Van Gogh turned to the Romantic idea that art could disclose the deep interconnections between people and nature and therefore could be a means of overcoming alienation and bringing about renewal.

DOI: 10.4324/9781003546856-4

But when his solitary sojourn in search of renewal in nature turned into a debilitating loneliness, he abandoned his Romantic dream and explored the consolations that art for its own sake could offer. In so doing, he gradually came to realize that art in itself is not enough, and in attempting to show how the aesthetic might point beyond itself to some further kind of gratification, he explored symbolic and expressionistic painting techniques which, in turn, fuelled his renewed interest in spirituality.

Throughout this journey, in which religion, morality and art remained complexly intertwined, Van Gogh struggled with his own profound personal experiences of alienation and *anomie*. He was outcast from his family. He was rejected by the Evangelical Committee that put an end to his pastoral endeavours in the Borinage. He was unable to fit into the academies where he attempted to study, and his sojourn in Paris, where he lived with his brother Theo, rapidly became a dysfunctional nightmare. He failed to set up a community of artists in Arles, where his personal relationship with Paul Gauguin ended badly, as had his earlier attempts at close personal relationships with women to whom he felt drawn, such as Kee Vos, Sien Hoornik and Margot Begemann. In Arles, the citizens saw to it that he was declared a public nuisance, and he voluntarily went to an asylum in St. Rémy, where he sympathized with the inmates, society's other marginalized and outcast unfortunates. His suicide then was the final expression of a profound, many-tentacled *anomie* that culminated in a self-destructive act, such as Durkheim indicated was one not-unlikely outcome of that condition.

Although Van Gogh's mental illness was not entirely attributable to the social conditions in which it became manifest, neither are the lines of separation clear, and towards the end of his life, he thought that the suffering he endured and against which he struggled in his painting was also the suffering of the era in which he lived. His personal *agon* was the *agon* of the times, a reflection of a whole era's way of thinking, a systemic *anomie*, and, as I mentioned in Chapter 3, he thought that "the impotence and imperfection of our works" (822/5, 153)[2] reflects the fact that society at large is in "a state of total laxity and anarchy" (655/4, 256).

Van Gogh's letters provide a powerful, often moving account of these developments, which cannot be well enough deduced from his graphic art alone. This is so because the letters provide information that the paintings do not – especially about his changing theories, opinions and aspirations. When his sister-in-law, Jo van Gogh-Bonger, set about promoting Vincent's work after he and Theo had died, she quickly realized that the letters and paintings belonged together, each enriching and illuminating the other.[3] Yet, for many years, the letters were treated as ancillary to the paintings, despite the fact that Van Gogh has been praised as amongst the greatest of Dutch writers. His correspondence has frequently been acknowledged as a literary achievement of the first order: "a literary monument of its own", "in the front rank of world literature" and so on.[4] The letters therefore have come late to the kind of critical assessment they deserve, but, most notably for the present purposes, as a literary achievement they enable us to share something of the felt complexities of the process of development through which Van Gogh's life and work recapitulate the cultural trajectory that led to the development of Modernism in his own time. And so, in the following pages, I focus on the letters. A further study would be needed to assess their complex continuities, as well as discontinuities, with his paintings and drawings.

In Chapter 3, I outlined the main phases of the broadly familiar unfolding of events from the Enlightenment to the Romantic movement and the late nineteenth-century cultural crisis that gave rise to Modernism, which, in turn, attempted to shape new modes of understanding and sensibility from within a fragmented tradition. I pointed out that, in order to do so, the new movement favoured oblique, experimental means of expression that would force readers and viewers actively to shape values that now needed to be produced rather than passively received.[5] In this context, Van Gogh occupies a highly interesting position between the challenges and struggles of High Victorianism and the revolutionary injunction to break from the old verities and to "make it new". The extraordinary fascination that his work exerts today is an expression, first, of his irreducible, special genius. But also, his work was shaped by the entire accumulated weight of the circumstances that gave form to his attitudes and practices, as well as by the hitherto unremarked fact that his development as an artist recapitulates a larger cultural narrative that, beginning from the early modern period, produced the secular society in which virtually every reader of this book now lives. Consequently, insofar as we are exposed, through Van Gogh's writings and paintings, to the larger processes at work in the shaping of a modern, secular identity, we are also encountering the story of ourselves, and the astonishing intensity of interest in Van Gogh today reflects in no small measure the fact that his art incorporates the narrative of our own historical becoming.

As we see, Van Gogh's changing views about religion and his continuing struggles with *anomie* are also central to this narrative. Like the great Victorians whom he admired, he was scathing about the shortcomings of the traditional Christianity of his upbringing. Yet, as he often remarks, he never relinquished his allegiance to the spirit of Jesus's teachings, and, eventually, he came to regard Jesus as the greatest of artists because he worked directly with people, creating them anew.[6] In making this claim, Van Gogh acknowledged that painting in itself could not show us how to live a full human life, a point that he confirms several times in his later letters, as we shall see. Likewise, the self-referential elements in his late paintings also draw our attention to the limits of artistic representation by thematizing the differences between art and life and the *aporia* to which he thus brings us in his late work is, for him, a precondition "from which a new religion, or rather, something altogether new, will be reborn" (686/4, 282). In the following pages, I deal mainly with the letters in order to explore the developments in Van Gogh's thinking that I have now briefly set out. In this exploration, his discussions of draughtsmanship provide a guiding thread because his changing attitudes to drawing so clearly epitomize the larger, more complex transformations under discussion.

The religious phase

Van Gogh's early letters from The Hague (1872–3) and from London (1873–5) express a homesick concern for his family as well as a buoyant enthusiasm about his aspiration to become, as he says, "a true cosmopolitan…with the world as my mother country" (18/1, 42). He read Michelet and Renan (33/1, 57), whose anticlerical opinions impressed him and he occasionally made sketches (32/1, 55). The counterpoint between homesickness and a rebellious sense of adventure in the early letters shows something of his fledgling state of mind, trying things out but anxious about surrendering well-established relationships and attachments. Also, notably, his first use of the coded word "it" appears in an early letter to describe the spark of insight or moment of revelation that great art expresses unaccountably and in excess of merely technical proficiency. Van Gogh picked up the term from his cousin, the painter Anton Mauve, from whom he would later take lessons. "As Mauve says – 'that's it'" he writes to Theo, and "that painting by Millet 'The evening angelus', 'that's it'. That's rich, that's poetry" (17/1, 41). Throughout his letters, Van Gogh emphasized how art makes familiar things appear in a new light, as if something vital and mysterious were emerging from the source of being itself. "It" is a shorthand reference to this experience, even though Van Gogh does not confine the word to art, as we shall see.

The early letters are often exuberant, but they are also without much critical reflection – they have buoyancy without gravity. "*Find things beautiful* as much as you can", Vincent advises Theo, because "most people *find too little beautiful*" (17/1, 41). "If one truly loves nature one finds beauty everywhere" (22/1, 45), and to "a good and a single eye…it's beautiful everywhere" (27/1, 5). Cruelty and injustice were not yet in the forefront of Van Gogh's mind, as they would soon enough become, and his description of what artists do is, likewise, confidently unproblematic: "painters understand nature and love it, and *teach us to see*" (17/1, 42), he writes, assuming a seamless continuity between what is seen and what is represented. Also, a general sense of ease, in these early letters, about the interrelationships amongst art, nature and religion reflects something of Van Gogh's upbringing in the parsonage at Zundert. Literature, painting and a love of nature were accommodated there to the moderate Calvinism of the Groningen School that shaped the thinking and sensibility of Vincent's parson father, Theodorus.[7] Erasmus was a formative influence on Groningen theology, and Erasmus had managed to maintain a broad, Pre-Reformation understanding of the continuity between art and theology. The Groningen School Calvinists were not nostalgic about Pre-Reformation religious orthodoxy, but the humanist principles of their great Dutch forbear encouraged them to mend some of the fracture lines between art, nature and religion that were insisted on by the Reformation as part of a rejection of the mythological and metaphysically based view of the world prevalent in the Middle Ages.

Van Gogh's early Groningen-influenced attitudes, together with his interest in becoming "a true cosmopolitan", took a sudden swerve in a conservative direction, however, when his fledgling career as an art dealer foundered and then collapsed. In 1869, he had joined the international firm, Goupil & Cie, in The Hague, but things did not go well, and after transfers to London and Paris he was fired by Boussod and Valadon, who had taken over from Goupil & Cie. In reaction, he declared, as it were, his own personal Reformation and decided to become a parson. Still, his new commitment to religion did not cause him to abandon his love for art, even though religion was now the pre-eminent concern and art was, at best, ancillary.

Van Gogh's religious phase began during his stay in Paris from 1875 to 1876, when he was still a Goupil employee. It continued during his sojourn in England from April to December, 1876 and his subsequent period in Dordrecht, where he worked in a stationer (kantoorboekhandel) from January to April, 1877. In Amsterdam, from 1877 to 1878, he undertook an ill-fated course of academic training in preparation for his candidacy as a parson, but he did not do well in his studies and went instead for a brief period of training in a missionary school in Brussels. Subsequently, from 1878 to 1881, he went to the coalmining district of the Borinage as an evangelist. His religious phase ended there when he realized that religion was not an effective remedy for the suffering and deprivation that he encountered amongst the Borinage miners.

Van Gogh's letters during his religious period declare his commitment straightforwardly and vigorously. Simply put, he wants to devote his life "to the service of Him and the gospel" (106/1, 149) and "faith in God is for me a certainty" (117/1, 164). By desiring to become a clergyman, he acknowledges that he is emulating his father, for whom he expresses unqualified admiration. "Men like Pa are purer than the sea", he writes, and his father's "countenance was like that of an angel" (87/1, 107) when he preached. Uncles Jan, Cor and Cent also have something spiritual about them, but "Pa has much more of it" (125/1, 184). And yet, even as he dedicates himself to his father's religion, Vincent registers a distinctive note of his own by emphasizing his concern for the poor. As so often in his career, the seeds of a future development were sown at an earlier stage, and his dedication to the poor in the Borinage would play a key role in turning him away from the traditional religious views of which, in the meantime, his father was the most admired living exemplar.

Van Gogh's letters from Paris at the beginning of his religious phase are notably more aware of the problem of suffering than was the case in his earlier correspondence. St. Paul's injunction (2 Cor. 6:10) to be "sorrowful, yet alway rejoicing" (35/1, 61) appears first in a letter from Paris, and thereafter Van Gogh uses it frequently. The two contrasting elements in St. Paul's verse catch the tension between Vincent's own optimism about the Christian good news and his increasing concerns about social injustice and the tragic side of life. "The Christian life", he writes, "has its dark side too", and so we must "take up our cross" and "follow Him", all the while remaining "sorrowful, yet alway rejoicing" (51/1, 75–6). The moving letters about the death of Van Gogh's friend, Harry Gladwell's 17-year-old sister, Susannah, and about a small boy who drowned in a canal, communicate a compassion that Vincent felt so deeply that he found himself struggling to contain it within a religious frame of reference. "God help us, struggling, to stay on top" (123/1:181), he writes to Theo, acknowledging the strain that he feels, even as he accepts the consolation that religion offers. His teacher in Amsterdam, Mendes da Costa, wrote that Van Gogh did not so much want to study as to "give peace to poor creatures and reconcile them to their existence here on earth"[8] (I, 169). This reconciliation was still primarily religious for Van Gogh, and the moral problem of suffering had not yet extinguished his conviction that "all things work together for good to them that love God" (40/1, 68). The Biblical promise "Behold, I make all things new" (101/1, 138), still contained a fundamental, vital hope as he shaped up to attending to the spiritual needs of the miners, whose lives he knew to be dangerous and difficult. Even so, in describing "the coal-miner is a type peculiar to the Borinage", he assures Theo that:

> The Belgian foreman has a cheerful character, he's used to this way of life, and when he goes down the pit, his hat topped with a little lamp whose job it is to guide him in the darkness, he entrusts himself to God Who sees his labours and Who protects him, his wife and his children.
>
> (148/1, 234)

This starry-eyed version of a devout miner protected by divine providence would not long survive Van Gogh's experience of actual miners, amongst whom he discovered that there was a good deal more cause for sorrow and a lot less for rejoicing. Earlier, in Amsterdam, he had written to Theo that "there is evil in the world and in ourselves, terrible things" and "without faith in a God one cannot live – cannot endure" (117/1, 164). Here, clearly, faith is a bulwark against despair, and this would not be the only time Vincent would resort to an ideal to protect himself from an unendurable reality. Not surprisingly, art also provided him with consolation, and the moment of epiphany that he often described as "it" is invoked again in the letters during Vincent's religious phase. A painting by Boughton is almost "it", "and yet that isn't *it* either" (44/1, 71), he writes. A discussion of Rembrandt and Maris leads to the assertion that "one finds *it* everywhere, the world is full of it" (120/1, 175). Here, interestingly, "it" refers to but is not confined to art as the reference extends also to special experiences in the world at large – moments when, as Van Gogh says elsewhere, "ordinary daily things make an extraordinary impression and seem to have a deep meaning in another setting" (129/1, 191). This broadened significance of "it" reflects Van Gogh's view of the world as an expression of God's design – a world in which art is valuable, even if subordinate to religion. And so, Vincent advises Theo to curtail his "feeling for art": "Don't give in to that too much" (49/1, 74), he writes. He even exhorts Theo to destroy his copies of Michelet and Renan and to be on guard against the poetry of Heine and Uhland on the grounds that "it's pretty dangerous stuff" (62/1, 85). Although these authors had influenced Vincent's own early, humanistic, "cosmopolitan" explorations, now, in light of his new, personal Reformation, he wants rid of them. Likewise, he refuses to praise a painting by Gerome because "I see not one sign of reason in it" (139/1, 215). And when he and his father visit a museum in Dordrecht to see pictures by Ary Scheffer, the religious content of the art was their main reason for doing so. The same priority holds when Vincent praises the preaching of Eliza Laurillard and Uncle Stricker. He compares them to artists (121/1, 178), but only because their art serves their religion.

Still, it is not difficult to detect an uncomfortable tension between Van Gogh's attraction to art and his conviction that he ought not to be too preoccupied with it. For instance, when he feels tempted to make some sketches, he checks himself on the grounds that "it would most likely keep me from my real work" and "it's better I don't begin" (148/1, 233). When he visited a Millet exhibition in Paris, he "felt something akin to: Put off thy shoes from off thy feet, for the place whereon thou standest is holy ground" (36/1, 62). The religious dimension of Millet's work no doubt makes the place holy, but is there not a suggestion here that the artist should also be a revered figure? In short, during Van Gogh's religious phase, art remained important, even as he insisted that religion came first. Art was not autonomous, but neither was it entirely suppressed.

Before I move to the crucial moment in the Borinage when Van Gogh discovered his vocation as an artist, I want briefly to take note of a further distinction that is relevant to the present discussion, and to which Van Gogh frequently returns. On a number of occasions, that is, he pauses to comment on the differences between a sincere religious commitment and a merely formalistic observance. For instance, he praises Uncle Stricker's preaching for "warmth and feeling" (121/1, 178) and for recommending "sincere religious feeling of the heart" in contrast to mere "outward forms and ceremonies" (122/1, 179). In a letter from Isleworth, he insisted that "one must have the gospel in his heart" (96/1, 126), and when he relented of his harsh opinion of Michelet, he did so because Michelet writes "from the heart in simplicity and with poverty of spirit" (143/1, 222). Only those who have "launched out into the deep sea of life", he goes on to say, can discover a sense of "the boundless and miraculous" (143/1, 223). And so, the preachers Laurillard and Stricker are like artists who are in touch with a creative inspiration that comes from the depths and is written in the heart, beyond prescription in keeping with the "avowal that all great men have expressed in their works" (143/1, 223). By contrast, those who practice only the "outward forms and ceremonies" (122/1, 179) miss the point of the religion they hold themselves to profess.

The differences between the spirit and the letter to which Van Gogh draws attention in these examples were to become urgent for him when he turned against conventional religion on the grounds that so often and so hypocritically preferred the letter to the spirit. And yet, the fact that he thought some Christians shared the same source of inspiration as artists also prepared the way for him to accord to art itself a quasi-religious function, however difficult it was for him to define what that function was.

During his religious phase, Van Gogh did not offer any radical critique of the religious tradition that was his birthright, but, in addition to his concerns about the spirit and the letter, several uneasy tensions in his letters during this period indicate the lines along which such a critique would develop. "It's important to hold on to what one has" (138/1, 213), he writes, but when his studies in Amsterdam floundered ("the worst time I've ever gone through" [154/1, 244] he would later tell Theo), he engaged in a flurry of map making (134, 136, 137, 138, 141), as if to chart some new course for himself. At the same time, he praised those who ventured "into the deep sea of life" (143/1, 223), suggesting that he was drawn to the unfamiliar and uncharted as a source of creative inspiration, even as he strove to "hold on to" his traditional convictions. Also, he knew very well that the "deep sea" can be dangerous and terrifying. "Misery and loathsome things" lurk all around, he writes, and some men and women "personify, as it were, the terror of the night". There are "things that have no name in any language" (144/1, 224) and are too deeply frightening for words. In such a terrifying world, religion offered a means of stabilizing one's self and of finding a way through the difficult terrain. But, then, also, creativity meant throwing the map away and plunging into the uncharted depths, risking its terrors while searching for its treasures.

In these letters, the tensions between a stabilizing, conventional religious observance and the ecstatic but terrifying depths are implicit rather than consciously developed, but the trajectory of Van Gogh's later career is already present in embryo, before he discovered where his own path lay. For now, art remained subordinate to his religious vocation, and although lines are detectable, they are not yet the open fractures they would soon become fault.

A change was underway, however, and Van Gogh knew it. For instance, he describes his experience in the Borinage as a time of "moulting" (155/1, 246), and the main agent in this process of transformation was his growing realization that religion did not offer a sufficient answer to the problem of suffering which, now, amongst the miners, he encountered in an all but unbearably immediate way. The sufferings and depredations that he now observed first hand gave him a very different view of the inhabitants of the Borinage than that expressed in his starry-eyed letter from Cuesmes. He was shocked to find that so "many people here are ill" (149/1, 236), afflicted by "typhus and virulent fever", "lying emaciated on their beds, weak and miserable" (151/1, 239). He discovered that the Marcasse mine has "a bad reputation because many die in it", and "the workers there are usually people, emaciated and pale owing to fever, who look exhausted and haggard, weather-beaten and prematurely old" (151/1, 239). Children, "both boys and girls" (151/1, 239), are put to work, and horses that are brought underground never see the light of day again (I, 187). In Van Gogh's descriptions of these shocking conditions, religion is no longer in the foreground, and the Biblical references and citations in the earlier letters from his religious phase dwindle and then stop. Instead, an intense moral imperative moves to the fore, as Van Gogh saw that people needed medicine and material care more urgently than they needed evangelization. Nonetheless, he still looked to Christ as "the great Man of Sorrows, who knows our diseases" (149/1, 236), and when Vincent's father visited, he and Vincent performed their pastoral duties together. He still admired art as "holy", and as a source of religious inspiration. "There's something of Rembrandt in the Gospels or of the Gospels in Rembrandt" (155/1, 247), he writes, and Tissot has something "great, immense, infinite" about him, and Meyron is, simply, "*Spirit*" (158/1, 257). Still, the centre of gravity was shifting, as Van Gogh acknowledged that his enthusiasm for the goals he once set for himself had "cooled considerably" (154/1, 244). He expressed reluctance about going home to visit his parents, and, in turn, his father expressed concern that Vincent's attention to the "sick and wounded" was distracting him from his religious vocation.[9] The members of the Evangelization Committee overseeing his performance as a lay evangelist apparently thought so too, and they fired him. The official reason was that he lacked organizational skills and did not speak well enough in public. Eventually, when his concerned family considered having him committed to a mental hospital, he broke off relations with them as well as with Theo, with whom he did not communicate for almost a year. In this broad context, Vincent decided that he wanted to draw the miners rather than preach to them.

Interestingly, when he arrived in the Borinage, Van Gogh remarked straight away that "there are no paintings here", and the people "haven't the slightest idea of what a painting is" (149/1, 236). As if to compensate, his letters supply a steady stream of references to many of his own favourite works of art. Then, as a response to the "extreme poverty" by which he found himself surrounded, his enduring interest in art prompted him to "pick up my pencil", and when he did so, he quickly understood that a radical change was taking place. Art enabled him to see with new eyes and to look at events "from a different perspective" (154/1, 244), and for the first time in his letters, artistic representation in itself is accorded special attention. "I know no better definition of the word *Art* than this: 'Art is man added to nature'", he writes, going on to explain that nature has a significance that "the artist brings out and to which he gives expression, which he sets free, which he unravels, releases, elucidates" and in so doing speaks "more clearly than nature itself" (152/1, 242). The relationship that Van Gogh describes here between art and nature marks a shift from his earlier, primarily religious view that "man is depraved by nature, at best a thief – but – with God's guidance and blessing he can become something of higher worth" (137/1, 212). This is a standard statement about nature and grace (the difference between our unregenerate and redeemed state), but when Van Gogh claims instead that the artist "sets free" what is confined in nature, it is as if the theological language about the economy of grace is transferred to the economy of art.

In response to feeling summoned to strike out in a new direction, Van Gogh undertook to illustrate the living conditions of the miners. Maris would make "a beautiful painting" of the Marcasse mine, Van Gogh writes, and, in imitation, he himself will "try and make a sketch of it to give you an idea of it" (151/1, 239). Before long, he was drawing "until late at night" (153/1, 243), and his former boss, Hermanus Tersteeg, sent him paints and a sketch book. "Already half full" (153/1, 243), Van Gogh reports, wondering at his own rapid pace of production. Drawing, not painting, was his main focus, and Tersteeg also sent a standard drawing manual by Charles Bargue, from which Van Gogh worked, he tells Theo, "from early in the morning until evening" (157/1, 253). Soon, drawing became something close to an obsession. Through it, "everything has changed for me" (158/1, 256), he writes, and, in addition, taking up his pencil helped him to alleviate a great amount of "discouragement" and to recover "my peace of mind" (158/1, 256).

Here, it is worth emphasizing the close connection between drawing and narrative in Van Gogh's new enterprise. That is, he wanted to record the wretched condition of the miners in order to tell a story that he was convinced was not well enough known. To this end, he hoped to sell his sketches (157/1, 253) and eventually to become "more or less capable in working in magazine or book illustration" (161/1, 263). The foundational role he accorded to drawing would remain at the forefront during Van Gogh's subsequent years in The Hague, when his passion for using his skill as a draughtsman to promote social reform was at its most intense. "For me it's a matter of learning to draw well" (158/1, 256), he writes, and "pure drawing" is "the foundation of all the rest" (246/2, 107) and "everything depends" on it (250/2, 115).

When he left the Borinage in 1880, despite his clearly stated misgivings, Van Gogh did in fact return to his parents' home in Etten. While he was there, he continued to draw, and he bought a copy of Cassagne's *Traité d'Aquarelle*, which he found especially helpful on the topic of perspective. He remarks that although Cassagne's main topic is watercolour, "I've been drawing with pencil only, worked up or heightened with the pen" (168/1, 275). And so, along with Bargue, whose exercises he still practiced (169/1, 275), Cassagne confirmed Van Gogh's dedication to drawing and to the narrative social commentary that drawing was well suited to promote. On his arrival in Etten, he straight away set about drawing woodcutters and their implements – "a cart, plough, harrow, wheelbarrow, etc. etc." (167/1, 275). As in the Borinage, his focus remained on the lives of working people. But, now the shift of emphasis from religion to morality also accelerated quite dramatically into a full-blown critique of the religious orthodoxy from which previously he had been reluctant to break entirely. For the first time, he describes his new order of priorities unambiguously: "God wants the world to be reformed by reforming morals" (187/1, 321).

An Enlightenment critique

The main catalyst for Van Gogh's change of emphasis from religion to morality was that, in Etten, Vincent met his widowed cousin, Kee Vos, with whom he fell catastrophically in love.[10] She, in turn, rejected him out of hand, and his family – his parents, Uncle Stricker (Kee's father) and Theo amongst them – did what they could to dissuade Vincent and to protect Kee from his embarrassingly importunate advances. Eventually, he acknowledged that the cause was lost, but he was devastated, and his letters to Theo about Kee are deeply painful. But his suffering also turned quickly to anger, as he blamed his parents' religious orthodoxy for preventing them from doing the morally right thing. "Love on" (180/1, 304) now became Vincent's rallying cry and "exchanging everything for everything is the real, true thing, that's *it*" (183/1, 312), he insists. The touchstone word "*it*", which Van Gogh had previously used in relation to art and religion, is now appropriated by morality, as Vincent became unrelenting in his criticism of his parents. "Whenever I tell Pa anything, it's all just idle talk to him" (193/I, 337), he complains. Although his parents might well read the Bible a great deal, they don't understand it at all (193/1, 337), and their way of living "would suffocate me" (193/1, 337). To further his argument, Vincent returned to Michelet, whose free-thinking opinions he threw in the teeth of his father in a way calculated to offend and shock. "If, for example, Pa sees me with a French book by Michelet or V. Hugo in my hand, he thinks of arsonists and murders and 'immorality'", but "I also told Pa frankly that in the circumstances I valued Michelet's advice more than his" (186/1, 317). For Vincent, Michelet is on the side of life and love in opposition to the "cold, hard, whitewashed church wall" (193/1, 338) behind which his cold and hard parents were sheltering. By contrast, love, as Michelet describes it, is "the most powerful" of "all powers", and Vincent suggests that Theo, too, would "benefit much more from re-reading Michelet than from the Bible" (189/1, 325). Here Vincent indicates – not without reason – that Theo was not sufficiently an ally in these reckless criticisms of their parents.

Still, despite his repudiation of the hard, whitewashed churches and their equally unappealing congregations, Vincent did not jettison what he took to be the core values of the religion of his upbringing. "I find the clergymen's

God as dead as a doornail. But does that make me an atheist?" (193/1, 340), he asks, and then answers:

> how could I feel love if I myself weren't alive and others weren't alive? And if we live, there's something wondrous about it. Call it God or human nature or what you will, but there's a certain something that I can't define in a system, even though it's very much alive and real, and you see, for me it's God or just as good as God.
>
> (193/1, 340)

The openness expressed here towards the encompassing mystery would eventually be expressed in Van Gogh's painting, but he had not yet become a painter, and, for now, in defiance of what he saw as the moral offensiveness of his parents' traditional religious observance, he raised what he called his "draughtsman's fist" (182/1, 308). This combative term is appropriate in the context of his undertaking to reform the world "by reforming morals" (187/1, 321), and, in addition, it confirms the close connection between drawing and social reform in his early work. Still, in Etten, Anton Mauve had also introduced Van Gogh to "tone and colour", even while encouraging him to go on drawing, with the expectation that the results would one day be "saleable" (193/1, 336). Mauve sent a paintbox, with paint and brushes, and Vincent looked forward to using them: but not yet. "We have to persevere, and now that I'm drawing figures I'll go on with that until I've made a good deal more progress" (177/1, 299). For now, that is, we "have to use that draughtsman's fist as best we can" (182/1, 309).

While Van Gogh continued to concentrate on drawing, his thinking about representation did not change. As we have seen, in the Borinage, he thought that art adds to nature and the artist works to put things "in a new light" (152/1, 242). He repeats this idea in Etten, arguing that whoever "wants sentiment in his work must feel it himself". And so, although there is "something stiff and severe in my drawings", he is convinced that Kee's loving influence will "soften" (185/1, 316) the harshness, so that the drawings will improve. In short, in a work of art, the artist's feelings are directly infused into what is produced, and this conviction would remain central to Van Gogh's thinking about representation until he discovered that colour could communicate independently of drawing and carried, as it were, an emotional charge of its own. But as long as the alignment of drawing and moral protest remained in the foreground, Van Gogh did not dwell on the more challenging aspects of the problem of how art represents reality. He had other things on his mind, not least amongst which was the fact that in The Hague he found a replacement for Kee in the unmarried, pregnant, part-time prostitute, Sien Hoornik. This scandalous offence to conventional mores caused such a storm of reaction within his family that Van Gogh dedicated himself even more fervently and indignantly to depicting the wretched lives of the poor and marginalized, with whom he now felt an ever-increasing solidarity. He insisted again that his parents' conventional religious observance betrayed the fundamental Christian message about love, and his resentment about his family's hostility to Sien was a main driver of his critique of religion, very much along Enlightenment lines, that came to a head in The Hague and consumed a great deal of his time and energy. Yet, Anton Mauve also had encouraged Van Gogh to become interested in colour and this suggestion gradually took hold. By the time he left The Hague and moved to Drenthe, painting had emerged as Van Gogh's main preoccupation. One result was that he came to a whole new understanding of the relationship between art and nature, and morality was no longer the main driving force behind his artistic endeavours. His Enlightenment critique of religion on moral grounds yielded then to a new, fundamentally Romantic, enthusiasm about the healing power of art and nature. But while he was in The Hague, the moral critique remained central, and was still closely tied to his disenchanted view of his parents' religion.

And so, Vincent's first letter to Theo from The Hague describes how difficult things were in Etten, and how, after a "violent argument" (194/2, 12), his father told him to leave. In a letter to his fellow artist Van Rappard, Van Gogh explained that he had trouble with his father "about all sorts of things", including "going to church" (195/2, 13) and yet, "at the back of it all", he assured Theo, was the "story of what happened this summer between me and K. V.". Again, the disagreement with his parents about religion was strongly connected to the moral challenges posed by Vincent's declaration of love for Kee. His response was, as ever, uncompromising: "I told Pa plainly that I found the whole system of that religion loathsome", and he is determined to keep clear of it "as against something fatal" (194/2, 12). At a later date, when his parents disapproved of an amorous relationship of Theo's, Vincent pounced again: they raise "this same objection", and "I find that unspeakably pretentious and utterly wicked. Ministers are in fact amongst the wickedest people in society, and barren materialists". In a case like Theo's, their parents' objections are "completely invalid morally", and refusing help to a woman because she is "poor and alone" is "inhuman…and doubly inhuman if a minister does it" (348/2, 341). Once more, morality is the standard against which religion is measured. And yet, as before, Van Gogh continued to affirm Jesus' teachings about love, and to gesture, vaguely, towards the existence of "something infinite" (259/2, 144), "something mysterious" (260/2, 145), "something precious, something noble, that can't be meant for the worms" (288/2, 208). Goya and Gavarni, whom Van Gogh admired, "both say '*Nada*'", but Van Gogh is different: "I can't sleep on that without having nightmares" (212/2, 44). Instead, he aligns himself with Thomas Carlyle, for whom mainline Christianity "lies in ruins, yet its sacred lamp is still burning" (356/2, 360). And, like Carlyle, Van Gogh remained drawn to "a certain man who wrote no books – i.e., Jesus" (325/2, 300). As with many other Victorians, including Van Gogh's favourites, Charles Dickens and George Eliot, Carlyle acknowledged that Christian values were part of the cultural fabric even as the authority of the institutional churches was on the wane. Writing about a traditional Christmas, Van Gogh advises "leaving aside" the question of "whether or not one agrees with the form". The important thing is "a feeling of belief in something on high even if I don't know exactly who or what will be there" (294/2, 223).

When Sien's baby was born, Vincent wrote to Theo that "it may be true that there is no God here, but there must be one not far off, and at such a moment one feels His presence" (245/2, 104). And at the height of his disappointment after Kee rejected him, he wrote:

> Now, as you know, I believe in God. I did not doubt the power of love. But then I felt something like, My God, my God, why hast thou forsaken me? And nothing made sense any more. I thought, have I deluded myself?… O God, there is no God!

Nonetheless, even though he felt that love "had been literally *beaten to death*", he held also that "after death one rises from the dead. Resurgam" (228/2, 74–5).

As I have mentioned, Van Gogh's attempts to describe the transcendent dimension in which he continued to believe remain vague, but it is worth noticing how he attempts to authenticate his intimations of the transcendent by grounding them in everyday experience, and how he looks to art to perform this function. For instance, to clarify what he means by "something on high", he points to the "unutterably moving quality that there can be in the expression of an old man", adding that "this is far from all theology" (288/2, 208). Throughout The Hague period, drawing remained his main instrument for capturing the "moving quality" of subjects such as the old man, together with a wide variety of poor people in whom he saw more genuine spirituality than in the whitewashed churches against which he so resolutely turned his back. During this time, he remained especially on the lookout for "what kind of drawings one might be able to sell to the illustrated magazines" (204/2, 28), and he even thought of returning to England to work for a magazine there (358/2, 265). To keep himself encouraged, he collected "almost the whole Graphic", a magazine that specialized in socially engaged drawings (331/2, 311) and that be described to Van Rappard as "a kind of Bible for an artist" (311/2, 266). Here, the religious dimension – the "something on high" – is manifest in the lives of ordinary people, especially the poor. In turn, Van Gogh hoped that drawing would bring his work to "the heart of the people" (226/2, 69), and, to this end, he looked for subjects "on wharves and in alleys and streets and inside houses, waiting rooms, even public houses". He declared that "one would rather be in the filthiest neighbourhood, provided there's something to draw, than at a tea party with nice ladies" (220/2, 57–9), and he imagined giving shelter to "a whole flock of poor folk for whom the studio could be a kind of harbour or refuge on cold days" (334/2, 320). These people's stories mattered to him, and the moral emphasis in his drawings drew heavily on their narrative content. Responsible drawing is like reading, Van Gogh argues, and "it's more or less the same with drawing as with writing" (265/2, 155). He explains to Van Rappard that "for me the English draughtsmen are what Dickens is in the sphere of literature" (267/2, 160), and "there's no other writer who's as much a painter and draughtsman as Dickens" (325/2, 300). A drawing by Van Rappard is "as if one were reading a description of a factory by Zola, or Daudet, or Lemmonier" (355/2, 358), and when Van Gogh describes his own drawing of poor people buying lottery tickets, he does not dwell on quality or technique, but on the story of the people who have bought a ticket "with pennies saved by going without food" (270/2, 168). His aim is not just to depict the scene, but to describe in a quasi-narrative fashion the misery of a whole way of life that calls for reform. The Bible was now validated for Van Gogh as a social gospel, represented by *The Graphic* and enacted by the morally vigorous, narrative structure of his drawings.

Still, as I have briefly mentioned, a counter-movement against Van Gogh's "Enlightenment" critique of religion and social hypocrisy was also taking place during his stay in The Hague, and eventually he would describe the change underway as a personal "revolution". The catalyst was "a certain feeling for colour" (371/2, 399) that he felt arising within him in sufficient force that he decided to switch his main focus from drawing to painting. The Hague letters provide helpful information about this awakening to colour, and, especially, how it came into conflict with his commitment to drawing.

Van Gogh's old boss and sometime benefactor, Hermanus Tersteeg, had already warned Vincent that his drawings were not saleable and he would do better as a watercolourist. Tersteeg's opinion was re-enforced by Mauve, and Vincent eventually came to see watercolour as a bridge between drawing and oil painting. For instance, watercolours can incorporate drawing, especially in ink, and Van Gogh thought that his watercolour experiments would make him a better draughtsman. When Tersteeg offered him a few small commissions, he asked for them "only in watercolour". In response, Van Gogh declared that "drawing is the most important thing, no matter what they say" (205/2, 29), and, later, when he experienced "a strong desire to paint" (248/1, 112), he pulled back, penitent: "I'm going to draw again regularly from morning till evening" (249/2, 113). "I also have nothing against making watercolours", he goes on, "but they're founded on drawing first" (252/2, 124). When, at last, he admits that he finds painting "very appealing" he quickly adds: "I've put a lot of work into drawing and will continue to do so, because it's the backbone of painting" (255/2, 130). In short, Van Gogh did not submit easily to the attractions of colour, one main reservation being that he thought his drawings would lose "their personal character if I attacked them with watercolour" (358/2, 365). While in The Hague, he also briefly explored oil painting, and on Theo's advice took himself to Scheveningen to paint seascapes. But after a brief period, he put his oils aside and, once more, returned to drawing.

Yet, the attractions of painting were steadily becoming less easy for Van Gogh to deflect. At first, he was tentative ("painting is not as alien to me as you might think" [255/2, 130]), and even plaintive ("I like painting so much" [363/2, 383]). He also complained that "paint is dear" (363/2, 283), as if trying to discourage himself even as he was cajoling Theo into covering the extra expense. Eventually, he complained that he had become burned out from too much drawing – "what they call dryness", he explains. When he goes on to suggest that "changing the manner of work and the subjects would be a good thing", it is hard to be sure how strategic his burnout self-diagnosis might have been, as a way of justifying his move away from drawing and towards painting. In any case, anticipation of the Romantic turn that was about to take place, he describes what sort of change he has in mind: "I need to look at length at things like the sea, the bronze potato leaves, stubble fields or ploughed earth" (365/2, 386). Above all, he declares, decisively, "the urgent thing for making progress this year will be that there must be painting" (366/2, 388).

As Van Gogh's interest in painting grew, he acknowledged that drawing was now on the back burner. With painting, "there's a kind of life that isn't due to accuracy of drawing" (371/2, 400), he writes, and, in a moment of impatience: "I don't give a rap if the drawing is erased". Rather, he pins his hopes on "plenty of painting this year" (370/2, 377), and he describes how, as a painter, he finds himself looking at his subjects differently, "through my eyelashes instead of looking sharply at the joints and analyzing how things fit together". This manner of looking through half-closed eyes enables him to see things "as patches of colour next to each other", so that the figure "isn't due to accuracy of drawing" but, rather, "the forms simplify themselves into patches of colour" (371/2, 400). Here, Van Gogh deliberately closes his eyes to the outlines and contours on which he had focussed so closely as a draughtsman. The "patches of colour" are now sufficient, and when he moved from The Hague to Drenthe, the "mysteriousness" (371/2, 400) of colour, as well as a new enthusiasm for painting, were his main sources of inspiration.

Almost as a corollary to this new privileging of colour over drawing, when he was faced with the choice between his commitment to Sien and his ambitions as a painter, Vincent close to abandon Sien. In so doing, he also abandoned his ambition to be an illustrator, and, as he himself realized all too well, his moral protests against injustice and lack of charity could now readily be turned against himself. The letters provide only hints of the pressure that Theo brought to bear on Vincent to disengage from Sien.[11] For his part, Vincent agonized about leaving her, and in Drenthe, he was haunted by a bad conscience. And so, as always for Van Gogh, moving on from the past did not mean abandoning it altogether. As we have seen, after he rejected official Christianity, some aspects of the old religion remained, as did his concern and sympathy for the poor – and for Sien – after he left The Hague. But neither religion nor social criticism was any longer a central preoccupation as he declared himself now to be, first and foremost, a painter.

During The Hague years, Van Gogh also maintained his earlier views on how artists transfer their emotions directly to the canvas when they paint. For instance, he explains that he could not have drawn "Sorrow" "if I didn't feel it myself" (217/2, 54), and in order to draw figures well, "one must have a warm sense within oneself" (277/2, 187). In a flush of enthusiasm, he assures Theo that Michelet "feels strongly, and what he feels he slaps on without troubling himself in the least about *how* he does it" (312/2, 268). Here, Van Gogh wants to draw attention to Michelet's over-hasty composition of *Le Peuple*, but he can't help admiring Michelet's spontaneity and ability to transfer his emotions directly onto the page. Along the same lines, when he moved to Drenthe, Van Gogh emphasized how "a power seething inside" (288/2, 209) had inspired him to go, and to be "far, far away in the country, far enough away for nature there to be real" (380/2, 414). The "drama" of the storm outside could then reverberate with the inner "drama of sorrow in life" (381/2, 415), and art could express this intense communion between humans and nature. As it happens, a similar, strongly expressivist view of art, whereby emotions are given shape in the work, lies at the very heart of the Romantic movement, the core values of which Van Gogh now embraced wholeheartedly.

Romantic self-fashioning and new challenges

One main intuition of Romanticism was that direct participation in nature is an antidote to the dehumanizing alienations caused by rapid industrialization. A healing re-integration with nature was thought necessary to counteract the instrumental attitudes, both to nature and to other people, that were producing increasingly obvious, harmful results. As the nineteenth century progressed, the damaging effects of industrialization were intensified by the infernal compact between the factory system of production and *laisse-faire* economics. As we have seen, Van Gogh was deeply concerned about the wretched lives of the urban poor in The Hague, and about the dehumanizing conditions of industrial production in the Borinage. In addition, he himself had laboured ceaselessly under the weight of an *anomie* that caused him to feel, as he says, "disenchanted" and engulfed by "a kind of emptiness which I can't fill with the things being made today" (280/2, 194). Even so, in Drenthe, he sought a renewal in nature that could be celebrated, above all, in colour, but, not surprisingly, traces of his earlier moral concerns remain, even though they are now in the background. He continued to be conscience-stricken about Sien (385/3, 12; 390/3, 21), and he still denounced his father as a "black ray" (388/3, 20), but, in Drenthe, his main focus was elsewhere. The Barbizon painters had declared, "I'm going to renew myself in nature", and Vincent assures Theo: "that's how I reason" (396/3, 38). He explains that the ocean brings up "something mightily serious" rising "from inside" (396/3, 38). "The heath speaks to you" and "you listen to that still voice of nature" which brings a "renewal of life" and "makes your whole nature different" (396/3, 39). The goal is "to refresh, to renew myself in nature" and to "have altogether new, firm ground beneath my feet" (403/3, 59).

In these confident assertions, Van Gogh repeats the core Romantic claim that people can be restored to a life-enhancing relationship with nature, and art can help to bring this restoration about. In counterpoint, Vincent casts the city-dwelling Theo in the role of an alienated victim of the dominant system. "You aren't part of nature", Vincent advises, combatively, and Theo would do better "to work at restoring the bond between yourself and nature" (394/3, 32). "So I say to you, plant yourself in the soil of Drenthe – you will sprout there. Don't shrivel up on the pavement" (400/3, 54). Real "contact with nature", Vincent goes on, is equivalent to "walking with God" and is totally unlike "the affairs of the big cities" (401/3, 56). In turn, this kind of contact "makes your whole nature different" and transforms your life and work (396/3, 39).

As is frequently the case in his correspondence, in these citations Vincent's strategies in dealing with Theo are not straightforward. Partly, Vincent wants his brother to appreciate and approve of the move to Drenthe. Also, to the extent that Theo might feel himself justly accused of conservatism and timidity, he might perhaps be more inclined to support Vincent's increasingly expensive painting habit. But there is a trace also of a further concern. On the face of it, Vincent's invitation to Theo to move to Drenthe and become a painter (a point on which Vincent is surprisingly insistent) was impractical. Besides, Vincent knew he would be sawing off the branch on which he was sitting, as far as financial support was concerned, but the fact is that he was desperately lonely. If the glory of being alone is solitude, and the pain of being alone is loneliness, then Vincent, contrary to his own expectations, was feeling a lot more pain than glory. He confides to Theo that he could deal with being short of money if he "weren't alone" (404/3, 61). Loneliness is a "singular torture", and being "absolutely cut off from the outside world" was becoming "enough to make me crazy" (408/3, 71). At last, when he could not stand the isolation any longer, he left Drenthe abruptly, and, as an inadvertent sign of his distress, the best solution he could devise was to return home to his parents.

By the time Van Gogh left Drenthe, painting was unequivocally in the foreground of his practice as an artist.[12] He had not given up drawing, but he was clear about the new order of priorities: "I'm drawing, but you know very well that painting must be the main thing as far as possible" (387/3, 16). Also, in his drawings, peasants now replaced the urban working poor of his earlier period. This typical Romantic shift of emphasis enabled him to focus on the endurance and authenticity of the working people rather than on the immiseration caused by industrial production and the kinds of social injustice that followed from it. In short, Van Gogh's earlier Enlightenment preoccupations were no longer a main concern as his personal, Romantic quest for renewal came into the ascendant. Not surprisingly, however, when he went to live with his parents in Nuenen, his experience was to be anything but a continuation of his Romantic interlude in Drenthe. Instead, for the next two years, he was thrown into a great deal of turmoil as he attempted to make sense of everything that had happened to him so far.

Initially, when he left Drenthe, the spirit of Van Gogh's Romantic interlude continued to buoy him up, and he reports how a six-hour walk across the heath "cheered me up no end". But almost immediately on his arrival in Nuenen he strikes a different note, explaining to Theo how "very loath" (409/3, 76) he is to be back living with his parents, and before long he was complaining bitterly that "it wasn't as lonely on the heath as it is in this house" (413/3, 81). Soon, the old grievances against his parents returned in force, embroiling Vincent once more in heated arguments about religion, morality and art. The letters from Nuenen are amongst the most conflicted and painful that he wrote, as he engaged for the last time in head-on conflict with his family. To counteract the stress, he worked feverishly, to the point where there were "many days when I'm relatively powerless. I can't eat and I can't sleep" (463/3, 175).

It is not surprising that the old disagreements about religion soon resurfaced in Nuenen, and with them, the well-tried recriminations from Vincent about his parents' disapproval of his relationship with Kee and Sien. When Theo, in turn, reproved Vincent for being too hard on their ageing father, Vincent turned on Theo as well, accusing him of following "in the footsteps of Pa, etc." (432/3, 115). He even caricatured Theo as "PA II" (474/3, 195) and castigated him for his hostile attitude to Sien and also for being insufficiently supportive of Vincent's work as an artist. The letters dealing with these quarrels show Vincent at his most pugnacious and disagreeable, but his troubles in Nuenen extended well beyond his family.

When his mother broke her leg, Vincent cared well for her, and when Margot Begemann, the 42-year-old, unmarried daughter of a prosperous Nuenen neighbour came to help, she and Vincent entered into some sort of amorous relationship, which ended up causing Margot so much distress that she attempted suicide by drinking arsenic. She survived, but was immediately spirited off to a hospital in Utrecht. Vincent's father then died suddenly, and Vincent was subjected to what he described as "absurd... reproaches" (490/3, 218) from his sisters, who probably – not without reason – accused him of contributing to his father's demise. As a result, Vincent left the parsonage under a cloud of acrimony. His approval rating soon fell even further when Gordina de Groot, one of his models, became pregnant and Vincent was suspected of being the father. He was not, but suspicions lingered. Finally, after a row with a local sacristan, Vincent had had enough, and, leaving a more than usual amount of wreckage in his wake, he set off for Antwerp.

In the turmoil of the Nuenen years, Van Gogh had found himself forced to re-assess the entire course of his career, and one indication of his conflict this caused him is an unusual recourse to binary opposites in his correspondence. Nowhere else in his letters do such strong polarizations express his divided state of mind so clearly. Thus, he finds Theo "very miserable", then immediately acknowledging "a good side" (which Vincent goes on shamelessly to describe as "your reliability with the money" [474/3, 194]). The brothers are "directly opposed to each other as enemies" on opposite sides of "a barricade" (461/3, 173). Theo has "two natures" (417/3, 90) struggling within him, and Vincent depicts him as "PA II", who threatens to initiate a "second series of quarrels" such as "I've had with PA I" (474/3, 195). He charges his father with being a "black ray" (415/3, 85), and even when he relents – claiming that "I also appreciate the good in Pa" – he quickly adds, "yet I think that Pa is *not good*" (415/3, 86). Paradoxically, he describes his father as "the most gentle of cruel men" (415/3, 86), and, for the first time, the old touchstone, "it", is used in an equivocal manner, as Van Gogh describes a "calm which is indeed *it* but far more still not yet it at all. What to do?" (415/3, 86). Here, the moment of epiphany is not clear, and Van Gogh does not know which way to turn – "What to do?" Elsewhere, he tells Theo, "we must split up" and "personally you're no use whatsoever to me" (474/3, 194). But then Vincent realized just as clearly that he needed Theo's "cooperation" and "friendship" (468/3, 184). In a moment of cruel duplicity, he told his father about a plan to go back to Sien and even "to marry her", but then admitted to Theo that he had no such plan at all. "Pa doesn't need to know this" (419/3, 93), Vincent confides. The callousness of this ruse aside, the admission suggests how fraught Vincent's state of mind was, as a host of traumas and failures, resentments and recriminations crowded back, making it difficult for him to find his bearings. He even considered going back to the Borinage to paint the miners (463/3, 176; 505/3, 245), and, perhaps while he was painting and drawing the Nuenen weavers, he recalled that in the Borinage he had once compared miners in their "cells" to weavers at their looms (151/1, 239). Now, he concluded that although the weavers were marginally better off, "all the same, it's often heart-rending here too", and the weavers are "as little cheerful as the cab-horses" (479/3, 201) in the mines.

As memories of Kee and Sien returned in force, Van Gogh even went to The Hague to re-visit Sien (416/3, 88), no doubt stirring up a lot of painful emotions. Also, he toyed again with the idea of making illustrations for magazines (463/3, 175), though he took no steps actually to do so. His Romantic aspirations in Drenthe in turn carried over to his conviction in Nuenen that "painting peasant life" benefits those "who think seriously about art" (497/3, 232). And in describing himself as "a peasant painter" (493/3, 225), he expressed a typically Romantic reverence for the people whose way of life he imagined as preserving an uninterrupted organic relationship with nature. And yet, in Nuenen, his own earlier attempt at Romantic self-fashioning had become just another element in a confusing detritus within which he felt unanchored and at sea as he sought to find a way forward now that God, Reason and Nature had proved, one by one, to be insufficiently sustaining.

Given the turmoil of the Nuenen letters, it is not easy to see which direction Van Gogh's art would now take. Yet, in retrospect, one event was decisive. That is, in Nuenen, he discovered Eugene Delacroix's theories about colour and was so taken by them that he never saw painting in the same way again. Briefly, from Delacroix Van Gogh discovered that the juxtaposition of colours within a painting produces an effect quite different from what we see if we consider the colours separately. Colours "which are very *luminous in the painting*", if "regarded *in themselves*" can, in fact, be a "*fairly dark, greyish tone*". For instance, a colour will appear "more or less red according to the colours that are next to it" (449/3, 155). In addition, Van Gogh found "the *laws* of colour" to be so "inexpressibly splendid precisely because they are NOT *coincidences*" (450/3, 156), and he cites Delacroix at length to explain the differences between primary and secondary colours, the complementary and contrasting effects of their juxtaposition, their degrees of brilliancy and the special effects of "broken tones". This new way of understanding in turn enabled Van Gogh to discover the extent to which his favourite painters do not reproduce the exact colours of the objects they depict. "Not one of them – the above-mentioned – are people who literally paint the local tone", but, rather, they "follow the spectrum they start with" in order to "carry through their own idea" (499/3, 235). From here, it was a short step to the conclusion that "COLOUR EXPRESSES SOMETHING IN ITSELF" (537/3, 303).

Van Gogh had long held that art is not just an accurate reproduction of appearances, but he had not previously described the distinction of a work of art in terms of juxtapositions of colours within it, without reference to the artist's intentions or feelings or to the actual colours of the objects being depicted. The implications of this new way of looking were as clear to him as they were startling: "a painter does well if he starts from the colours on his palette instead of starting from the colours in nature" (537/3, 302). Consequently, when he shifted his attention away from the Romantic idealism of his sojourn in Drenthe in order to focus on the aesthetic by way of Delacroix's colour theory, Van Gogh found himself considering how far a work of art could go in foregrounding its own internal strategies. In a postscript to a letter to Theo, Vincent praises Poussin as a painter who "makes one think about everything", and in whose paintings "all reality is also symbolic" (533/3, 288). The word "symbolic" had not yet come to mean as much to Van Gogh as it would in the following years. Still, he was beginning to understand in a new way that the meaning of a painting can be enhanced by deliberate departures from direct representation, even though he resisted removing painting too far from a recognizable, common world. Throughout his career he insisted on working from actual scenes and from models, rather than from imagination or "memory", and in Arles, his conviction about this point lay at the core of his quarrel with Paul Gauguin. Afterwards, as his mental health deteriorated, the prospect of losing contact with the everyday material world – whether in actuality or in painting – became especially threatening. In turn, his struggle to resolve the tension between symbolism and direct representation was the matrix within which he also finally located the question of religion – a location in which it has remained for a great many people ever since.

As colour appeared in a new light, Van Gogh began to show an interest in Impressionism, even if only to admit that it is "not entirely clear to me what one should understand by it" (450/3, 156). Some weeks later, he writes again: "there's a school – I believe – of impressionists. But I don't know much about it" (495/3, 228). And yet, he had already grasped one main aspect of Impressionism when he wrote that "the best paintings" when "seen from close to are touches of colour next to one another, and create their effect at a certain distance" (539/3, 309). Also, in Nuenen, he repeated his earlier point that he liked to look through half-closed eyes in order to see patterns of colour rather than outlines (499/3, 234). This, again, is not far removed from Impressionism, even as Van Gogh acknowledged that "here in Holland it's hard to work out what Impressionism is actually trying to say" (467/3, 182). In fact, while he was in Nuenen, his painting practice remained very much in his Dutch mode, and he even predicted that his palette would "become slightly more sombre rather than lighter" (467/3, 182), citing the "very dark" (499/3, 233) *Potato Eaters* as an example. And so, he wanted his palette to become darker, even as his admiration for Delacroix and his tentative curiosity about Impressionism were pointing in the opposite direction. He would have to go to Paris – by way of Antwerp – and then Arles, to discover the real implications of Impressionism for his work.

When Van Gogh arrived in Antwerp, he was enthralled by the energy and diversity that he found there, and how dramatically the "incomprehensible confusion" (545/3, 323) of the docks and quays stood in contrast to "the tranquillity of a country village" (545/3, 323) such as Nuenen. Amongst much else, he took special note of a pervasive fashion for "Japonaiserie", a cultural trend imported especially from Paris. Van Gogh interpreted this cultural phenomenon loosely to describe exotic and novel effects in general: "*Japonaiseries*. I mean, the figures there are always in motion, one sees them in the most peculiar settings, everything fantastic, and interesting contrasts keep appearing of their own accord" (545/3, 323). He began collecting Japanese prints, even though the full impact of Japanese art did not yet register on him as it would later in Paris and Arles. He was too busy on too many fronts to focus exclusively on Japanese art, as he visited dance halls, bars and museums and was constantly on the search for models. He was also beset by health problems. He had bad teeth, ten of which he had removed, and he suffered from a stomach disorder (550/3, 333). Often, he went without food because he spent his money on models. Then, as if to steady himself and bring some order into his life, he enrolled in the Koninklijke Academie (the Antwerp Academy of Art). Initially, his impressions were favourable:

> I've been painting there for a few days now and it suits me very well. Above all because there are all sorts of painters there, and I see them working in very diverse ways – something I've never had – often seeing other people at work.
>
> (554/3, 342)

But, as ever, the contrarian in Van Gogh lurked not far off and soon emerged, presenting itself an all too characteristic combativeness: "I think that the fellows in the drawing class *all* work badly and in completely the wrong way" (554/3, 342), he writes, indignantly, to Theo. In turn, accounts by his fellow students confirm what a cause of consternation Van Gogh was and how "very soon the news spread like wildfire all over the building complex that some sort of savage had dropped in", upsetting "the director, the drawing master and the pupils".[13] Moreover, this new, disruptive student's painting was judged incompetent by his teachers and he was sent down to a junior drawing class. This relegation must have been especially wounding because in the previous years Van Gogh had worked so hard on his drawing, and because he had looked so contemptuously on the drawings of his fellow students whose skills were now judged superior to his own. He strove to save face with Theo by stating only that he was now drawing again and that he planned to keep doing so for another year. He did not mention being sent to the lower class,[14] but he admits that, now, "*I see my own mistakes*. That's a great help in overcoming them" (557/3, 346). Nonetheless, it was not long before he got back to telling "some of the fellows, that their drawings were completely wrong" (559/3, 350).

Clearly, Van Gogh did not have much of a future at the Academy, and, as with his criticism of religion, his main objection to academic institutions was that their dogmatism destroyed the spirit without which art could not flourish. In a colourful, earlier letter (881) to Van Rappard, he distinguishes between two sorts of mistress. The first, "Dame Nature or Reality", is fruitful and "your true love"; the second, to whom the Academy is compared, is treacherous and false. These false mistresses are "women of marble – sphinx – cold vipers – who would like to bind men to themselves, entirely". They "suck your blood" and "*freeze* men, and *petrify* them" (184/1, 313). Similar accusations of hardness, freezing and petrification had been directed by Vincent against his religiously orthodox parents, and the analogies between his hostility to religious and academic institutions are clear. And so, when he writes to Theo about the Academy, he could well be writing about institutional religion. "And you really should see!!! how flat, how dead and how bloody boring the results of that system are. Oh, I tell you, I'm very glad to have seen it properly at close quarters" (561/3, 353).

And yet, Van Gogh's love of art was, if anything, intensified by his experience at the Academy, which thrust his interest in the aesthetic even more emphatically into the centre of his concerns. "More and more", he writes, "I imagine that in the end art for art's sake – working for the sake of working – energy for energy's sake – really becomes very important to all the good fellows" (557/3, 347). He did not waver, either, in his conviction that colour could best express the essential "energy" he admired, and Delacroix remained his main inspiration. Contrary to fashion, Delacroix tried "to get people to believe in the symphonies of the colours" (552/3, 339), just as Van Gogh also was intent on doing. Consequently, he found himself increasingly interested in the internal dynamics of the artifact, and with its simultaneous likeness and unlikeness to the world it depicts.

Van Gogh's brief, three-month stay in Antwerp was a bridge between the two main phases of his career, the first of which took place in the Netherlands and the second in France. In Antwerp, he had dropped several hints about moving to Paris (551/3, 338; 555/3, 343; 557/3, 346), and in February, 1886, he arrived there, unannounced. Initially, he proposed spending a year at Fernand Cormon's studio in order to study drawing. It is hard to know if he was still sensitive to the judgement of his Antwerp teachers that he did not draw well, or if he wanted to suggest a low-key plan to Theo, stressing continuity and allaying alarm about how precipitously he had turned up on Theo's doorstep. As it turned out, Theo had a good deal to be alarmed about, and Vincent's drawing project seems not to have gone far, if it got underway at all. He seems mainly to have painted at Cormon's, and to have caused much the same consternation there as had greeted his similar, spectacularly chaotic efforts in Antwerp.[15] In a letter to the English painter, Horace Mann Livens, written soon after he arrived in Paris, Van Gogh insisted that "true drawing is modelling with colour" (569/3, 364) and, despite his more modest assurances to Theo about wanting to draw, his real goal was to explore the expressive power of paint, as Delacroix had advised. To this end, his actual practice at Cormon's turned out to be less important than the people he met there. Henri de Toulouse-Lautrec, Louis Anquetin and Émile Bernard also were Cormon's students, and Van Gogh soon extended his circle of acquaintances to include Paul Signac, Edgar Degas, Paul Gauguin and George Seurat. In short, he found himself at the centre of the most creative movement in European painting at the time, and he soon tried his hand at a variety of the new styles and techniques to which he was exposed.

Paris, Arles and St. Rémy: the "draughtsman's fist" recovered

When Van Gogh arrived in Paris, in 1886, the eighth Impressionist Exhibition was under way. The first had taken place in 1874, and now, more than a decade later, a younger group of painters was experimenting with a variety of new techniques. In his letter to Livens, Van Gogh is already aware that Impressionism was on the point of becoming passé: "since I saw the Impressionists I assure you that neither your colour nor mine as it is developing itself, is *exactly* the same as their theories" (569/3, 364). Nonetheless, Van Gogh experimented with Impressionist techniques, as he did also with pointillisme and the new, emergent "cloisonnism" pioneered by Bernard and Anquetin. Also, he and Theo were avid collectors of Japanese prints, and Vincent was soon reproducing elements of Japanese colour and composition in his paintings. In addition, he tried his hand at a wide variety of subjects: landscapes, flowers, scenes from Montmartre, old boots, self-portraits and portraits of other people. His palette brightened even as darker shadows were being cast across Vincent's life as his inexhaustible energy spilled over into furious rows with Theo and equally furious bouts of drinking. Eventually, he seems to have realized that his way of living was unsustainable and he decided, abruptly as ever, to move on. Later, looking back at his time in Paris, he would draw a distinction between the Impressionists of what he called the "grand Boulevard" and those of the "Petit Boulevard" (584/4, 24).[16] The first comprised older, established figures such as Pierre Auguste Renoir, Claude Monet and Alfred Sisley. The second was made up of Van Gogh's new acquaintances – Toulouse-Lautrec, Anquetin, Bernard and Gauguin. "I really am an Impressionist of the Petit Boulevard" (592/4, 42), he writes, declaring his allegiance to the younger group who were exploring ways to take painting beyond the shimmering depictions of light and colour that characterized the painters of the Grand Boulevard. And so, a course of development was set in motion that, in the broader history of art, would lead through symbolism to expressionism and abstractionism, and in so doing would focus increasingly on the non-representational. In Van Gogh's immediate circle, Toulouse Lautrec had already combined drawing and painting in a new, stylized manner that, as Julian Bell explains, Van Gogh had never before seen.[17] Emile Bernard and Louis Anquetin were experimenting with cloisonnism – a painterly imitation of stained glass, with separate compartments (cloisons) of colour set apart by heavy lines, just as segments of coloured glass in stained glass windows are connected by strips of lead. On another front, Paul Gauguin introduced visionary and dream elements into otherwise realistic settings, and the currently fashionable *Japonaiserie* also did much to shape the experiments of the younger painters. Van Gogh writes about how Anquetin and Bernard were immersed in "the Japanese style" (620/4, 110), which he also briefly summarizes: "the Japanese disregards reflection, placing his solid tints one beside the other – characteristic lines naively marking off movements or shapes" (621/4, 113). As he goes on to point out, the Japanese print makers placed a heavy emphasis on drawing and on areas of flat colour, and to that extent they resembled cloisonnism. In addition, they favoured compositions with bold diagonals, unexpected cropping and unusual perspective lines. To the extent that Van Gogh was influenced by these techniques, drawing became much more marked in his painting,[18] and, in turn, this development helped to further his interest in the non-realistic aspects of artistic representation, until, eventually, he found himself confronting the limits of the aesthetic itself. In turn, this confrontation constituted an aporia within which his most fully developed understanding of religion took shape.

In Arles, which Van Gogh fondly imagined as "the equivalent of Japan" (620/4, 110), colour was, again, his over-riding preoccupation: "I believe in the absolute necessity of a new art of colour" (585/4, 26), he writes, and "the painter of the future" will be "a colourist such as there hasn't been before" (604/4, 76). And yet, he found himself looking also for something beyond colour as he became increasingly convinced that the revolution introduced by the Impressionists did not go far enough: "it won't be Impressionism that will formulate the doctrine" (683/4, 276), he assures Theo. His longstanding theory that an artist does not simply reproduce appearances became intensified in Arles to the point where he deliberately introduced distortion and exaggeration into his paintings with a view to drawing attention to how he was intent on breaking with realism. He cites with approval the preface to Guy de Maupassant's *Pierre et Jean* commending "the freedom the artist has to exaggerate" in order to create a "more beautiful, simpler, more consoling nature" (588/4, 30). Later, he explains: "I'm trying now to exaggerate the essence of things, and to deliberately leave vague what's commonplace" (613/4, 94), and he writes about his portrait of Eugène Boch that "I'm now going to be an arbitrary colourist. I exaggerate the blond of the hair, I come to orange tones, chromes, pale lemon" (663/4, 237). Along similar lines, he claims that Monticelli "neither pretends to give us, local colour or even local truth" (598/4, 60), and "from the point of view of the reality of things", Monet does not follow the "*laws* of nature" (650/4, 200). For his own part, he wants to carry his "experiments" in painting even "further", so that colour "isn't locally true from the realist point of view" (676/4, 260). In so doing, he aims to produce much more exaggerated effects than in his previous paintings. His portrait of a Zouave is "a coarse combination of disparate tones that isn't easy to handle" (629/4, 142), and the "Sower" and "Night Café" are "exaggerated" to the point that they seem "atrociously ugly and bad" (680/4, 268). He wants to get the "*music* of local colour" into "La Berceuse" and yet "it's badly painted, and chromos bought at the penny bazaar are infinitely better painted technically, but all the same" (745/4, 406). Self-consciously bad painting, ugliness and harshness are now part of the effect, and, as the words "but all the same" suggest, he intends the apparently descriptive faults to be an expressive enhancement. But how much deliberate ugliness can a painting stand in the name of expressive power? Van Gogh had long toyed with the idea that good painting has some imperfection built into it,[19] and now he suggests that the deliberately non-realist elements of a painting can be especially effective in awakening us from the everyday deceptions that we have normalized. This is a bold development, and the path that brought him to it lay to a great extent by way of Japan, or, rather, what he took Japan to be.

In Arles, Van Gogh writes, "I feel I'm in Japan" (585/4, 26) and it is not necessary to travel abroad because "the equivalent of Japan" (620/4, 110) already exists in the South of France. Also, when he declares "we love Japanese painting", he adds that "all the Impressionists have that in common" (620/4, 110). For Van Gogh, that is, Japan was a place of the mind, a way of seeing that he regarded as integral to Impressionism and to the artists of the Petit Boulevard. He cites an article describing Anquetin as "the leader of a new movement in which Japonisme" was especially marked, adding that "young Bernard has perhaps gone further than Anquetin in the Japanese style" (620/4, 110). Writing about an unsuccessful exhibition of Japanese prints that he organized at the Café Tambourin in Paris, Vincent assures Theo that it "had quite an influence on Anquetin and Bernard" (640/4, 174), and about a visit to Sigfried Bing, a Parisian dealer who specialized in Japanese prints, he writes that "I learned there myself, and I got Anquetin and Bernard to learn with me" (642/4, 178). He refers, unproblematically, to "the French Japanese the Impressionists" (642/4, 177) and to the assumption that "Japanese art, in decline in its own country, is taking new roots among French Impressionist artists" (640/4, 175). These extravagant claims can help to clarify how Japan itself was not so important for Van Gogh as how the idea of Japan enabled the Petit Boulevard painters to further their experimental goals. Indeed, Van Gogh's ideas about Japan became so enmeshed with his practice that he concluded: "all my work is based to some extent on Japanese art" (640/4, 175). There is no way to make sufficient sense of this statement unless "Japanese art" stands for a range of practices that were taking Van Gogh beyond the techniques and conventions to which he was accustomed as be sought, together with his Petit Boulevard companions, to discover a new, symbolic language for painting. In this spirit, for example, he wanted his painting of his bedroom to suggest "*rest* or *of sleep* in general", and to that end, he explains how "the shadows and cast shadows are removed: it's coloured in flat, plain tints like Japanese prints" (705/4, 330). Here, the aim is to go beyond a realistic depiction of the interior scene in order to evoke a quality of "inviolable rest". To create that effect, as he says, he drew on the example of the Japanese print makers and painted his bedroom without shadows and with uniform, flat colours that would have the desired calming effect. And yet, the bedroom is not at all as restful as Van Gogh says it is; rather, it is strangely agitated, paradoxically ambivalent, single yet double, lonely yet consoling – an evocation not just of sleep but of an unease and restlessness that sleep might temporarily allay. Van Gogh did not derive these effects from the Japanese prints, but, instead, the Japanese prints were a catalyst for his own creativity. By and by, when he found that he had no further use for the catalyst, references to Japan in his correspondence fell away almost entirely.[20]

A further, significant consequence of Van Gogh's interest in Japanese prints was that, under their influence, drawing took on a new importance for him. As we have seen, the pre-eminence he accorded to drawing during his Enlightenment phase was supplanted by colour during his period of Romantic self-fashioning. But drawing acquired a new importance when Van Gogh began increasingly to explore non-realistic painting techniques, and, to that end, he drew on the Japanese practice of combining drawing and colour. Even after his enthusiasm for Japan had waned, he continued to resort to heavily drawn outlines, sharply defined, curious perspectives and precisely drawn details.

In Arles, to help with the revival of his drawing skills, Vincent asked Theo to send him a copy of Cassagne's *ABCD Du Dessin* (630/4, 150) to help with drawing lessons that he was giving to a Zouave lieutenant at the time. But Van Gogh also connected the book directly to Japan, explaining that he now had "an ENORMOUS amount of drawing to do, because I'd like to do drawings in the style of Japanese prints" (594/4, 48). Later, he goes on to say that he wants "to do some pen drawings …coloured in flat tints like Japanese prints" (614/4, 95), and he admires how "the Japanese draws quickly, very quickly, like a flash of lightning" (620/4, 110). In St. Rémy, he confirmed that he "came to the south" to get "a more accurate idea of the Japanese way of feeling and drawing", which he wished to combine with what he learned about colour from Delacroix (801/5, 89). This combination was Van Gogh's way of participating in the experimentalism of the Petit Boulevard, even as he hesitated to push his ventures too far into non-realism. As ever, he was curtailed by the old anxiety about losing contact with the common world under the influence of an insufficiently restrained imagination. With these considerations in mind, he perceptively identified a key tension in his own work between "something that really exists" and some further, non-material significance:

> I'm still between two currents of ideas, the first, material difficulties, turning this way and that to build up an existence and then the study of colour. I still have hopes of finding something there. To express the love of two lovers through a marriage of two complementary colours, their mixture and their contrasts, the mysterious vibrations of adjacent tones. To express the thought of a forehead through the radiance of a light tone on a dark background. To express hope through some star. The ardour of living being through the rays of a setting sun. That's certainly not *trompe-l'doeil* realism, but isn't it something that really exists?
>
> (673/4, 255)

The "two currents of thought" with which the passage begins deal with a tension between supplying Van Gogh's material needs on the one hand, and his creative enterprise as a painter on the other. This tension then passes over to a discussion of how painting is a means of insight into the non-material aspects of people's lives, and yet, such insight cannot be disconnected from the material objects through which it is disclosed.[21] In Arles and St. Rémy, Van Gogh thought quite a lot about this kind of question. In Arles, Paul Gauguin brought it to the surface in an especially challenging way.

In contrast to Van Gogh, Gauguin recommended allowing the imagination a great deal of freedom, and after registering an impression of a scene in *plein air*, he liked to complete the painting in his studio, often altering it and introducing motifs from dream or mythology to enrich the composition. Van Gogh initially tried to follow Gauguin's example while the two men lived and worked together in Arles: "I don't find it disagreeable to try to work from the imagination" (723/4, 367), Vincent explains to Theo, and "Gauguin gives me courage to imagine, and the things of the imagination do indeed take on a more mysterious character" (719/4, 356). Again, Vincent writes to his sister Willemien that Gauguin "encourages me a lot often to work purely from the imagination" (720/4, 360), and paintings such as *Reminiscence of the Garden at Etten* and *Woman Reading a Novel* show Gauguin's influence quite clearly. But Van Gogh's compliance with Gauguin's advice did not last long and took an abrupt about-turn after an argument that resulted in the deranged episode in December, 1888, when Vincent severed part of his left ear, almost bled to death, and was confined in hospital. His summary of the main disagreement with Gauguin goes directly to the point: "I believed him led by his imagination, by pride perhaps but – quite irresponsible" (736/4, 388).

Van Gogh's hostility towards the man he once revered is partly explained by the fact that Vincent came to realize that his tastes, favourite artists and preferred way to work were very different from Gauguin's. In addition, as we have seen, Van Gogh was worried about his mental stability, a point to which he returns frequently in his letters from Arles and St. Rémy. With the onset of his mental illness, he knew too well that his imagination could run amok and plunge him into delusions and hallucinations. Now that the "unbearable hallucinations" have calmed down and become "a simple nightmare", he writes, he can work again – "unless", that is, "my work is yet another hallucination". "I'll send you what I've promised you from the beginning" he assures Theo, "if I'm not mad" (743/4, 402), and during one of his crises, "it seemed to me that everything I was imagining was reality" (760/4, 430). In short, Van Gogh knew that, for him, the lines between imagination and reality were easily blurred, and he feared the consequences. And so, in his painting, his interest in transfiguring the ordinary world through imagination is counteracted by his need to stay anchored in a recognizable, everyday reality. This tension had played a role in his thinking about art from the beginning of his career, but now, in a greatly intensified form, it became the crucible within which his great, last paintings took shape. In addition, during this period of intense creativity, Van Gogh became increasingly aware of the limitations of painting to effect the kinds of change that he had once hoped that religion, morality and nature could effect. "This artistic life", he writes, is not "*the* real one" (602/4, 73). Rather, "*people* are the root of everything" and "it would be better to work in flesh itself than colour or plaster, in the sense that it would be better to make children than to make paintings" (595/4, 50). "Why am I so little an artist", he asks himself, "that I always regret that the statue, the painting, aren't alive?" (659/4, 227–8). "The more I think about it", he goes on, "the more I feel that there's nothing more genuinely artistic than to love people" (682/4, 272). "You see what I've found, my work", he writes to Wil, "and you also see what I haven't found, everything else that's part of life" (626/4, 130).

In declarations such as these, Van Gogh acknowledges that there are more important things in life than art, and, not surprisingly, in seeking to bridge the gap between art and life, he looked towards religion. One, not very realistic way in which he did so was to propose founding a quasi-religious community of artists, so that the deficiencies of art would be compensated by the human community of creative people working together. Gauguin's arrival in Arles was to be a step towards establishing such a community, which Van Gogh imagined along religious lines. "When it's a matter of several painters living communally", he writes, "I stipulate first and foremost that there would have to be a father superior to impose order, and that naturally that would be Gauguin". Theo, who was unable to live in Arles, would be included as "one of the first apostle-dealers" (694/4, 302). Tongue-in-cheek as these suggestions are, they are not entirely flippant, and Van Gogh is quite serious in declaring the value of "living more or less like monks or hermits with work as our ruling passion" (660/4, 235). Already, he feels that he has within himself "something of a dual nature, something of both the monk and the painter" (708/4, 336), and "if I were a Catholic I could resort to making a monk of myself" (751/4, 416). He admires the Japanese artists for living "a brotherly life" (696/4, 308), and "isn't it almost a new religion that these Japanese teach us" (686/4, 282), he asks, going on then to paint a self-portrait as a Japanese monk: "a bonze, a simple worshipper of the eternal Buddha" (695/4, 304).

Van Gogh's aspirations to found a quasi-religious community of artists were hardly destined to work out, and there are enough wry touches in his writing to suggest that he took his own recommendations with a pinch of salt. Still, the idea had some real appeal for him, and the desire that fuelled it is expressed also in the other main way he sought to bridge the gap between art and life – namely, a revival of his old theory that art points towards an encompassing mystery, and in so doing performs a quasi-religious function.

As was the case since the end of his early religious phase, Van Gogh continued to hold that traditional Christianity did not meet the demands of the times. To clarify the point, he writes to Theo from Arles about an old woman whom he imagines as "tormented in the Christian system". Although her experience of Christianity is oppressive, the old woman's intuitions of a future life and her "instinctive belief in an '*it's there*'" (656/4, 220) are valid and important. Here, the talisman word, "it", is given a religious rather than an aesthetic meaning, as Van Gogh again found himself considering the claims religion might still have on him. He even tried to make a painting of Christ in the Garden of Olives, but failed. He tried again, with the same result. In keeping with his thoughts about the old woman's intuition that "*it's there*" he turned his attention then to Tolstoi, who focussed on what is "eternally true in the religion of Christ, and what all religions have in common" (686/4, 280). For Van Gogh, Tolstoi was the harbinger of a whole new kind of spiritual understanding: "something altogether new, will be reborn, which will have no name but which will have the same effect of consoling, of making life possible, that the Christian religion once had" (686/4, 282). Like Tolstoi, Van Gogh therefore found himself drawn to the perennial truths of Christianity and he focussed on the figure of Jesus as a way of recovering the older forms of a "Christian religion" that had once given comfort to a great many people, but no longer did so.

In keeping with his observation that the new, Tolstoi-inspired religious sensibility has "no name", Van Gogh returns to the same vague gestures towards an encompassing mystery that we have seen in his earlier letters. "In life and in painting too I can easily do without the dear Lord", he writes, "but I can't, suffering as I do, do without something greater than myself" (673/4, 253). When he paints people, he wants to show something "of the eternal, of which the halo used to be the symbol" (673/4, 253), and painting "gives me a sense of the infinite". He imagines "another, second hemisphere, invisible, it's true, but where we arrive when we breathe our last" (652/4, 204), and, already from the beginning, a child in a cradle has "the infinite in its eyes" (656/4, 220). He explains to Émile Bernard that "I could hardly give a damn about the *veracity* of the colour" of a particular painting, provided that the painting evokes the "yearnings for that infinite of which the Sower, the sheaf, are the symbols" (628/4, 137). Here, the symbolic dimension of the painting stimulates a religious longing that points beyond the painting to a condition in which the something new with "no name" might be encountered. Interestingly, in this context, Van Gogh accords Christ a special status as a bridge between art and religion, explaining to Bernard that Christ was "*an artist greater than all artists*" because he worked "*in* LIVING FLESH". That is, Christ "made neither statues nor paintings nor even books...he states it loud and clear...he made...LIVING men" (632/4, 154). Again, Christ "is more of an artist than the artists" because "he makes men instead of statues" (633/4, 157).

Despite the relegation of his own kind of art to an inferior status when compared to Christ's, Van Gogh was encouraged by the fact that the symbol of St. Luke, patron saint of painters, is an ox. Like an ox, Van Gogh was determined to plod on patiently, even though he felt that the conditions under which artists were constrained to operate in the modern world were all but intolerable, as he felt himself "stagnating under the stupefying yoke of the difficulties of a craft almost impossible to practice on this so hostile planet, on the surface of which 'love of art makes one lose real love'" (632/4, 155). These bitter words express a deep discouragement, as Van Gogh confronted the possibility that painting is futile in a world that had so effectively dislocated art from more fulfilling and sustaining kinds of human relationships. The letters provide several striking examples of feelings of isolation, rootlessness and estrangement characteristic of *anomie*. "At present…we're sailing on the high seas in our small and wretched boats, isolated on the great waves of our time" (643/4, 179), and in contrast to an "architecturally constructed" medieval society, "we're in a state of total laxity and anarchy" (655/4, 216), so that the best that artists can do today is to "paint an *atom* of chaos" (655/4, 218). Later, in St. Rémy, he wrote to Bernard that "modern reality has such a hold on us" that we are thrown back "forcibly into personal sensations" and isolated within a society that "makes existence very hard for us". One result is the "impotence and the imperfection of our works" (822/5, 153).

The emphasis in these passages falls heavily on dislocation and rootlessness in a society where common bonds have been lost and where the atomized individual is adrift without bearings. Art, then, is constrained to mirror the prevailing fragmentation, giving rise to a sense of no way out, the *aporia* that caused Van Gogh to try to recover a sense of "the infinite", and of "something greater than myself" (673/4, 253), as the insufficiencies of his work as a painter increasingly bore down on him. "Painting", he writes, is not "the same as having a child", which "I've always thought…was the most natural and best thing" (885/5, 260). "I still love art", he assures Theo, but he regrets not "having a wife of my own" (896/5, 286). And, "yes, there's something in life other than paintings", and if we neglect that further dimension, "nature seems to avenge itself" (820/5, 142). Still, even in the face of these realizations, Van Gogh knew that, come what may, he would remain an artist. Painting "occupies and distracts me – which I need very much" (782/5, 37), he writes, and "work distracts me infinitely better than anything else" (798/5, 72). He paints in order to "console" (782/5, 38) and, not least, "to console myself" (805/5, 101). This combination of distraction and consolation indicates how art played a therapeutic role for Van Gogh as his mental health declined and he feared the hallucinations that threatened to detach him from the everyday world. The great paintings of his last years were produced from a tension between a tenacious contact with the material, everyday actuality and a visionary radiance intimating an encompassing mystery. In his exploration of new techniques for depicting this visionary concreteness more effectively, Van Gogh looked to drawing to help him to produce expressive distortions of everyday reality within a painting, while also continuing to describe the contours of a familiar world.

After he left Arles, Japan was a less pressing concern for Van Gogh, but in St. Rémy he continued to acknowledge his indebtedness to "the Japanese way of feeling and drawing" (801/5, 89), and he describes his painting "Entrance to a Quarry" as being "like a Japanese thing", going on to emphasize the special distinction of "Japanese drawings" (810/5, 118) in general. In recalling his indebtedness to Gauguin, he specifically notes that he owes "a lot to things that Gauguin told me as regards drawing" (849/5, 193), and he praises

Bernard for having "found perfect things" as far as an expressive "drawing style" (816/5, 134–5) is concerned.

The significance of drawing in these references to Japan, Gauguin and Bernard can best be understood in the context of Van Gogh's exploration of stylized effects. Theo was well aware of the direction in which his brother was headed when he compared Vincent's work with the efforts of painters "who occupy themselves seeking the symbol by dint of torturing the form". "But how hard your mind must have worked", Theo goes on, "and how you endangered yourself to the extreme point where vertigo is inevitable". Theo then cautiously suggests that Vincent should proceed carefully, because "before your complete recovery you mustn't put yourself at risk in these mysterious regions, which it appears one can touch lightly but not enter with impunity" (781/5, 36). In these cautionary messages, Theo saw clearly that Vincent was pushing traditional techniques to the limit, but he also worried that Vincent's mental health would suffer because "you have endangered yourself to the extreme point", and here he mirrors an anxiety of Vincent's own. In his reply, Vincent agrees that he feels

> greatly driven to seek style, if you like, but I mean by that a more manly and a more deliberate drawing. If that will make me more like Bernard or Gauguin, I can't do anything about it. But I am inclined to believe that in the long run you'd get used to it.
>
> (816/5, 134)

Here, Vincent agrees that he is engaged in a search for "style", and he insists, specifically, that this search entails "a more manly and a more deliberate drawing" which, in turn, he associates with Bernard and Gauguin. In this context, it is helpful also to consider Van Gogh's references to Egyptian art, especially in his later letters. The "Egyptian artists", he writes, "express all these intangible things: goodness, infinite patience, wisdom, serenity, with a few masterly curves and marvellous proportions". That is, drawing can evoke qualities such as kindness, wisdom, patience and serenity, not by way of narrative illustration, but by how the lines and curves are deployed so that "the thing depicted and the manner of depicting it are in accord" (778/5, 31). Reflecting on his paintings of cypresses, Van Gogh explains that he wants them to be "like the canvases of the sunflowers", adding that a cypress "is beautiful as regards lines and proportions, like an Egyptian obelisk" (783/5, 46). Although, as in his sunflower paintings, he remains a colourist, now in his cypresses he looks also to the stylized, heavily drawn contours of Egyptian art as an example of the new kind of effects he wants to produce.[22] As James Hall points out, Van Gogh's "obeliscal" trees are stable, protective and architectonic, as well as full of vital energy – qualities that Van Gogh sought in order to counteract incoherence and rootlessness, while remaining creative. As Louis Van Tilborgh explains, in his late work Van Gogh increasingly deployed "graphic representation, determined by line, which is sometimes painterly, sometimes more drawing-like". The resultant, "almost stenographic rendering of reality", was as James Hall suggests about the "obeliscal" effects, a means of suggesting a new kind of social order informed by a new "spiritual component", as Van Tilborgh points out.[23] For his part, Van Gogh hoped that other painters would explore the same kind of "symbolic language" (RM 21/5, 231), and his paintings of olive trees are a further example of what he recommends. They are "exaggerations from the point of view of the arrangement, their lines are contorted like those of the ancient woodcuts" (805/5, 101), and yet, in a painting "where these lines are close together and deliberate", the effect is enhanced even if it is "exaggerated" (805/5, 104). And so, in the paintings of olive trees, as with the cypresses, a deliberate and close attention to drawing is integral to how colour reaches towards an enhanced intensity and suggestiveness.

Émile Bernard's cloisons and the stylized contours of Egyptian art therefore helped Van Gogh better understand how drawing within a painting can open the viewer up to much more than a merely accurate reproduction of appearances. Again and again in the late paintings, an array of stylized deformations paradoxically returns us to things we thought we already knew, and which now are transfigured, radiantly intense even as they remain recognizable objects from the everyday world. Maintaining an equilibrium between the ordinary and the transfigured presented considerable challenges, especially as Van Gogh struggled with mental illness in St. Rémy, where, to make matters worse, the old-fashioned religious questions returned to plague him in a new and frightening form. He describes how he was afflicted by "mixed-up, atrocious religious ideas" such as "I never had in my head in the north" (805/5, 100). He has "crises like a superstitious person would have", and he wonders if, perhaps, he has been living in the old cloisters for too long (the Saint-Paul-de-Mausole Asylum had once been a monastery) (805/5, 100). He cannot grasp why his illness has taken such "an absurd religious turn" (801/5, 89), especially given the fact that he is "horrified by all religious exaggeration" (801/5, 94), and he declares himself determined to leave the asylum "immediately, without giving a reason" (805/5, 105) if he should suffer another, similar attack.

These unsettling experiences certainly did not incline Van Gogh to think any more favourably about the traditional Christianity he had long since rejected, but nonetheless they belong within the broader narrative of his increasing interest in religion during the last two years of his life. His aspiration towards the new religion with "no name", his imagined quasi-religious community in Arles, his description of Christ as the greatest of artists and his ideas about a renovated "obeliscal" society point towards a kind of renewal in which tradition could be reshaped to meet the needs of the present cultural phase. In September, 1889, commenting on "La Berceuse", he remarks that he would have liked to make portraits "of saints and of holy women from life, and who would have appeared to be from another century and they would be citizens of the present day, and yet would have had something in common with very primitive Christians" (801/5, 92). Here, a combination of ancient and modern evokes a primitive Christian simplicity appropriate for the present day, without being explicitly religious in a traditional way. When he attempted but failed to paint Christ in the Garden of Olives, Van Gogh settled for painting just the garden, and he did so with the intent that "the olive picking as it's still seen today" would "perhaps make people think" of the Biblical scene "all the same" (820/5, 144). That is, in excluding any explicit Christian reference, he allows a figural suggestiveness to evoke Christ's ordeal. Like Christ, the olive trees are at once tormented, enduring, and life-affirming, and modern people will identify with this struggle even if they have discarded traditional Christianity. Van Gogh's resort to these kinds of figural effects without explicit reference to traditional religion is complemented by his use of broad gestures to indicate the encompassing mystery. Thus, he admires "that glimpse of a superhuman infinite" (784/5, 49) in Rembrandt, and wonders about "a vague probability that on the other side of life we'll glimpse justifications for pain" (784/5, 53), as he looks towards "a ray from on high which doesn't belong to us" as a precondition of making "beautiful things" (850/5, 195). In allowing glimpses into the overarching mystery, painting provides consolation in the face of life's terrors, but art does not prescribe any kind of ontological commitment, and, for Van Gogh, the figural stops short of the doctrinal. Jesus is exemplary because he was a higher kind of artist and not because he founded a church. Moreover, in re-creating human beings, Jesus' art also shows the limitations of other, lesser kinds of art, so that art's transfigurative agency has to be measured against art's insufficiency.

Conclusion

I have suggested that the course of Van Gogh's personal development duplicates the larger course of the development of Western culture from the beginnings of the modern era in the period of the Scientific Revolution and Protestant Reformation to the Modernist movement of the late nineteenth and early twentieth centuries, and that Van Gogh's extraordinary impact today remains bound up, however tacitly, with the fact that his work is an *anamnesis*, an ingathering of the main crises in the unfolding of this larger history.

To summarize: Van Gogh's early upbringing took place within a moderate, Reformed tradition in which art, nature and religion were mutually reenforcing in a manner that retained something of a pre-Reformation, Erasmian way of thinking and understanding. His turn towards a more radical religious position – his personal Reformation – was followed by a disappointment that led to a vehement counter-reaction against orthodox Christianity. This counter-reaction was based on moral principles and was conducted much in the spirit of the eighteenth-century Enlightenment critique of religion. When his attempts to effect moral and social reform failed to produce the results he wanted, Van Gogh resorted then to a period of Romantic self-fashioning by way of a solitary communion with nature. But, again, he was disappointed, and he sought consolation in painting for its own sake. By and by, however, his realization of the limitations of the aesthetic caused him to be more acutely aware of the differences between art and life. His painting then became increasingly self-reflexive, thematizing its revelatory power and its limitations simultaneously, as a means of celebrating the world of ordinary experience while also pointing beyond it.

And so, in the course of his career Van Gogh discovered how traditional ideas about God, Reason and Nature were no longer sustaining, and he realized that the new movements in art underway at the end of the nineteenth century could not fully supply the deficit. And yet, he came to realize also that art was well ordered to give form to the crisis itself and to enable a better understanding of the struggle for value from within the pervasive *anomie* which he endured personally and considered to be a sign of the times in which he lived.

In resisting the commodification and instrumentalizing of human relationships brought about by mass industrialization, a main strategy of Modernist art was to make itself difficult of access by thematizing its own procedures and materials. In so doing, it resorted to discontinuity and the disruption of conventional forms of representation in ways that required a high degree of participation on the part of readers or viewers. New values and meanings now needed to be actively constructed rather than passively received, and readers and viewers would discover that although value is hard won, it is worth the effort. The High Modernists knew that they were demanding a lot, and, in the upshot, their project did not sufficiently prevail against the juggernaut of commodity culture and the political order supporting it. For those inclined to remain sceptical about values in general, a smart deconstructionist intervention could show that value-claims are relative, or a means of exercising power. Consequently, freed from old-fashioned constraints about conforming to received standards, art could celebrate the commodity cornucopia itself, value-free and inspired by a spirit of play, taking pleasure in the game for its own sake. The sensibility emergent from these attitudes and preferences is what is meant by postmodernism, and its exposures of the subterfuges of power and the hypocrisies of established authority are frequently liberating and non-elitist. And yet, the degree to which postmodernism has intensified an already widespread sense of rootlessness and disorientation is also significant. Today, Spinoza's bad dream of an infinite series in perpetual motion, an unstable reiteration without foundations, has become normalized.

One main aspect of Van Gogh's story, as I have described it, is, then, that it is not just his story. It is the story of all of us who live in or are otherwise shaped by the secular society and who are part of the larger historical narrative of its emergence whether we recognize it or not. This narrative does not indicate any single trajectory forward; rather, the core values that marked its emergence remain with us, neither universally authoritative nor entirely emptied of content. Traditional religion is still an option; the Enlightenment critique remains relevant; Romantic views of an organic re-integration with nature are salutary; art is valued and its achievements held in high esteem. On the one hand, then, we are presented with an embarrassment of riches, a cornucopia of options. On the other hand, today these options are all too readily regarded as commodities circulating in an endless process of exchange, without stable meaning or enduring communal significance, so that the very liberties we celebrate engender the *anomie* that corrodes them. In this broad context, Van Gogh's painting and writing remain as a protest declared out of the heart of his personal tragedy, and his work as a whole offers a restorative, life affirming vision that is also an antidote to the *anomie* which he experienced directly and which he describes through a powerfully rendered, personal recapitulation of the historical process of its emergence. No address to questions about spiritual consolation and the place of religion in society today can well avoid the complexities, insights and challenges with which Van Gogh's life and work present us, and which remain constitutive of the postmodern condition itself.

Notes

1 I deal with these interconnections in *The Letters of Vincent van Gogh. A Critical Study* (Edmonton: Athabasca University Press, 2014), pp. 23–69.

2 All citations from the letters are from *Vincent van Gogh: The Letters*, ed. Leo Jansen, Hans Luijten, and Nienke Bakker, 6 vols (New York and London: Thames and Hudson, 2009). Letter numbers are cited in the text, with the volume and page number following the forward slash. An expanded version on which the printed edition is based is available free of charge at www.vangoghletters.org.

3 For an account of how Jo promoted Van Gogh after his death by exhibiting and selectively selling his paintings and publishing his letters, which she used also in support of the paintings, and vice versa, see Hans Luijten, *Jo van Gogh-Bonger. The Woman Who Made Vincent Famous*, trans. Lynne Richards (London: Bloomsbury, 2023; first published, *Alles voor Vincent*, 2019). Leo Jansen points out that Vincent's brother Theo gave excerpts of the letters to critics to enable them better to understand the paintings. See Leo Jansen, *Van Gogh and His Letters* (Amsterdam: Van Gogh Museum, 2007), p. 42.

4 See Jansen, *Van Gogh and His Letters*, p. 5; *Vincent van Gogh. Ever Yours. The Essential Letters*, ed. Leo Jansen, Hans Luijten, and Nienke Bakker (New Haven and London: Yale University Press, 2014), p. 38: "his letters were recognized as literary texts in their own right" and are "a highlight of world literature". The Museum of Dutch Literature places Van Gogh amongst the top one hundred Dutch writers. See *The Letters of Vincent van Gogh. A Critical Study*, p. 7 and p. 222, note 12. Dick van Halsema "Vincent van Gogh: A 'Great Dutch Writer' (between Marcellus Emants and Willem Kloos)", in *Van Gogh: New Findings*, ed. Chris Stolwijk, *Van Gogh Studies* 4 (Zwolle: Wbooks; Amsterdam: Van Gogh Museum, 2012), p. 19.

5 This is a key point in Nothrop Frye, *The Modern Century* (Toronto: New Edition, Oxford University Press, 1991), pp. 25ff., *et passim*.

6 See Letter 632/4, 154. I return to this topic later in the chapter.

7 For an account of the Groningen and Modern schools of theology, which were favoured, respectively, by Vincent's father and his Uncle Stricker, see Tsukasa Kōdera, *Vincent van Gogh. Christianity Versus Nature* (Amsterdam and Philadelphia: John Benjamins Publishing Company, 1990), pp. 19 ff.

8 *The Complete Letters of Vincent van Gogh.* Introduction by V. W. Van Gogh; preface and memoir by Jo van Gogh-Bonger, 3 vols (Boston: Little, Brown and Co., first published 1958, 3rd edition, 2000), I, 69.

9 Cited in Steven Naifeh and Gregory White Smith, *Van Gogh: The Life* (New York: Random House, 2011), p. 199.

10 Vincent had met Kee briefly in Amsterdam in 1878. See *The Letters of Vincent van Gogh. A Critical Study*, p. 39.

11 Amongst other indications is Vincent's referring to Sien as "the woman", no doubt following Theo's instruction not to use her name. See also, for example, 248/2, 112 ("I'll go along with what you think as far as I can"); 253/2, 126 (on talking "as agreed not about special matters"); 301/2, 234 ("You said to me then, don't marry her"); 432/2, 114 ("So you got your way regarding the woman").

12 Naifeh and Smith, *Van Gogh: The Life*, p. 313, claim that Van Gogh's discovery in Drenthe of "how persuasive paint could be" was "a turning point for Vincent and for Western art".

13 See *The Complete Letters*, II, p. 506.

14 On Vincent's evasions, see Naifeh and Smith, *Van Gogh: The Life*, pp. 482 ff.

15 See Naifeh and Smith, *Van Gogh: The Life*, pp. 510 ff.

16 For an account of the distinction and the context within which it developed, see Julian Bell, *Van Gogh. A Power Seething* (Boston, NY: New Harvest, Houghton Mifflin Harcourt, 2015), pp. 83 ff.

17 *Van Gogh. A Power Seething*, p. 82.

18 See further, Louis van Tilborgh, *Van Gogh and Japan* (Amsterdam: Van Gogh Museum, 2006). Also, *Van Gogh and Japan*, ed. Louis van Tilborgh, Nienke Bakker, Cornelia Homburg, Tsukara Kōdera, Chris Uhlenbeck, with a contribution by Claire Guitton (Amsterdam: Van Gogh Museum, 2018) contains a helpful collection of essays.

19 See further, *The Letters of Vincent van Gogh. A Critical Study*, pp. 52 ff.

20 Louis van Tilborgh, *Van Gogh and Japan*, p. 7.

21 Other commentators describe this effect in various ways. Deborah Silverman suggests "sacred realism", in "Framing art and sacred realism: Van Gogh's ways of seeing Arles", *Van Gogh and Gauguin: The Search for Sacred Art* (New York: Farrar, Straus and Giroux, 2000), pp. 45 ff. W. H. Auden describes Van Gogh as making paintings "which should be religious and yet contain no traditional religious iconography". See *Forewords and Afterwords*, ed. Edward Mendelson (New York: Random House, 1973; first published, 1959), p. 299. Adam Gopnik praises Van Gogh's "visionary dailiness". See "Van Gogh's ear. The Christmas Eve that changed modern art", *New Yorker*, Jan. 4, 2010, p. 54.

22 See James Hall's two-part article, "Becoming 'obeliscical': Van Gogh, ancient Egypt and the global Orient – I: figures", *The Burlington Magazine*, 165, March, 2023, pp. 280–301, and "II: obelisks", April, 2023, pp. 394–411. Hall distinguishes between two main phases in Van Gogh's allusions to ancient Egypt. The first deals with references to the Sphinx, and has a mainly psychological significance. The second deals with obelisks and is especially pertinent to Van Gogh's later interest in architectonic, stable, and creative societies, in contrast to the incoherence and rootlessness of his own times. See p. 411 for comments on the cypresses.

23 Louis van Tilborgh, "Vincent Van Gogh's Final Months", in *Van Gogh in Auvers sur Oise. His Final Months*, ed. Nienke Bakker, Emmanuel Coquery, Teio Meedendorp, and Louis van Tilborgh (Amsterdam: Van Gogh Museum, 2023), p. 25.

5 Conclusion

Modernity, Modernism and the Religious Question

In the previous chapters, I have suggested that *anomie*, by which I mean a condition marked by fragmentation, isolation and a loss of shared purpose and meaning, is widespread in modern Western secular societies. I have suggested also that the causes of this condition are embedded in the development of secularism itself. That is, with the emergence of a neutral state untrammeled by traditional religious obligations, state power was directed increasingly to the protection of a dominant capitalist economy to which competitive individualism and self-interest were, as they remain, indispensable. Whatever traditional trappings might be carried over from the past would now be ornamental, perhaps even a useful distraction. But the core function of the secular state would remain unaltered, however much tempered in the interests of restraining capitalism's most egregious excesses. Although capitalism has been revolutionary in bringing immense material benefits to a great many people, it also has brought immiseration to a great many others and, from within itself it is incapable of developing countermeasures to offset the exploitation and inequalities that it inevitably produces. An endless cycle of production, consumption and competitiveness pre-empts whatever shared understandings and values would promote solidarity and reciprocation in the quest for a common good. These are not its business. Instead, by pitting each against all in the drive to get ahead, capitalism promotes a hyper-individualism that is inherently divisive and isolating, and which, combined with the complexities introduced by the shift from industrial capitalism to financial capitalism, has resulted in the "crisis of incoherence" described by Bellah. In turn, in the present postmodern cultural phase, this crisis is greatly intensified by the digital communications revolution, even as its extraordinary, exponentially expanding advances have brought immeasurable benefits. Nonetheless, it is also the case that immediate access to an overwhelming surplus of information, misinformation and disinformation imposes severe burdens on assessment and assimilation for a great many people, giving rise to widespread feelings of confusion, powerlessness and frustration. Again, these further fragmentations within secularism have developed from freedoms that secularism itself has pioneered.

DOI: 10.4324/9781003546856-5

First amongst these was freedom of religion, and from the start, Spinoza saw clearly how a critique of religion was the necessary underpinning for a political philosophy promoting democracy. In the same spirit, secularism today maintains a separation of church and state and considers religion a private matter. One result is that endless varieties of religion are on offer today for private consumption, as many-hued and novel as the free market itself. In *The Modern Century,* Northrop Frye argues that the governing modern mythology privileges openness, and because this is so, imagination takes on a special role in the immense range of religious choices that are now so readily available. As we have seen, at the advent of Modernism, art itself for Van Gogh had acquired a quasi-religious status, and today many people continue to find art a sufficiently convincing representation of the human condition. But for those who are drawn to take a step further in declaring a religious commitment, the imaginative power of the tradition to which they are drawn, whether as new or established believers, is likely to play a significant role. This does not mean that religion is reducible to art: religion prescribes specific beliefs and a way of living, and art does not, and a viable religion today can be expected to promote a way of life based on equality and the irreducible dignity of each human person. In so doing, it will draw on a complex cultural tradition with a strong narrative identity as it offers an *anamnesis* returning us to the mystery of origins as it also addresses the mystery of ends, the overarching matter of our ultimate concerns.

The *anamnesis* that religions provide in evoking the mystery of origins takes different symbolic and narrative forms in different cultures. In the Preface, I suggested that no single cultural narrative accounts for the complexity of the phenomena to be explained; so also, no religious tradition today can credibly claim to have complete and exclusive access to truth. And yet, different religions can reveal truths about ourselves, our relations with each other, with the world and the cosmos that are valuable for negotiating the crises of life and in shaping life-affirming and stabilizing attitudes towards the mystery of existence itself. In so doing, not all religions are of equal value and relevance, but, as I indicated in Chapter 1, they all have in common a dependency on language, a fact that, in turn, makes inter-religious dialogue possible.

In Chapter 1, I described language itself as a complex phenomenon, a mosaic of strategies, sometimes synergistic, sometimes at odds, and the languages we speak today are the product of a complex, layered evolution, containing within itself cries, gestures, mimetic displays, story-telling, symbolism as well as conceptual argument. Each of these components fulfils a certain potential and answers a specific need, and in order not to distort what it means to be a person whose identity is shaped by and embedded in language, a developed religious tradition will represent how the entire, complex course of our linguistic evolution remains present as a prior condition of whatever transformations and insights a religious view of the world might effect. Not every religious tradition, however, has equivalent persuasive power in a different cultural context, if only because a language that we do not understand well does not affect us as profoundly as does the language that has done most to shape our identity. And yet, especially today, openness to traditions other than our own authenticates our adequate understanding of the tradition to which we happen to belong. Otherwise, dialogue cannot take place, and the dismal history of religions that insist on excluding and denouncing each other need not be rehearsed here.

With these points in mind, in the previous chapters I have followed one strand within the story of Western secularism, with a view to assessing some consequences of that development for the status of religion today. In so doing, I have suggested that *anomie* is a consequence of the emergence of Modernism from Modernity, which is to say the profound and far-reaching changes initiated by the Protestant Reformation and the Scientific Revolution of the sixteenth and seventeenth centuries.

In dealing with the beginnings of Modernity, I take Spinoza as a representative figure on the grounds that his main arguments are uncannily prescient about how enlightened reasonableness, democracy, universal rights and religious toleration, together with a radical critique of the Bible and traditional ideas about God, would mark the development of the secular age in which we now live. In his own time, Spinoza was a disruptive and alarming figure, as he systematically dispensed with the Biblical creator God, sin, hell, heaven, free will and divine providence. His demystifications of these traditional beliefs and concepts had enduring consequences in the fields of religion (which he saw largely as a manipulation of people's hopes and fears), epistemology (he discarded traditional metaphysics as fictive, at best) and politics (in promoting democracy he called in question traditional power structures, especially those supported by religious claims). In addition, by challenging religion to live up to its main injunction to love our neighbour, Spinoza presented morality as a benchmark for assessing what is important in religion in general, based on universal "laws of human nature". And in asserting that God is accessible to everyone and every religious tradition, he promoted a "manner of living" based on a moral concern for others, in contrast to what he saw as the obfuscations, superstitions and manipulations of those who remain "captive to myth", and for whom religion is doctrinaire, exclusivist, and an instrument for political control. This aspect of Spinoza's thought remains powerfully relevant today, even though it encounters many of the same kinds of resistance as it did during his own time. Nonetheless, an acknowledgement that fundamental moral truths are shared by the world's major religions is now broadly accepted as an indispensable foundation for a rapprochement between those traditions, which might then adjust to one another's perspectives and correct one another's inadequacies through a network of exchanges convergent upon the mystery of existence that no religion fully contains but which each addresses within a specific cultural situation. The universal principles to which Spinoza points – love your neighbour and acknowledge that "my being and perfection depend entirely on your perfection" – therefore remain a core challenge for traditional religions attempting to find common ground while preserving cultural differences. Today, it is more than ever the case that people do not find their way to a religious view of the world by conforming *a priori* to traditional rules and practices. Rather, they are more likely to discover how traditional rules and practices help them better understand their human condition while promoting a universally humanizing view of the world.

In arguing for the pursuit of truth for its own sake, preferably in the company of like-minded companions who share the recommended "manner of living" in a communal "spirit", Spinoza points towards what Balibar calls a "transindividual" mode of understanding. In so doing, Spinoza also proposes that we move beyond a childish phase of simple egoism, through a stage of enlightened self-interest, and, finally, to a "rebirth" leading beyond selfishness. Here, it is worth noticing that although Spinoza rejected Medieval metaphysics, he remained a metaphysician himself, especially in his doctrine of the single Substance and its corollaries. In addition, he did not fully anticipate how his own critique of the medieval, "realist" view of universals, which he saw as a fanciful confusion of words and things, would be used against his own idea of the one Substance, his philosophical God. For Spinoza, a world without God would be meaningless – indeed, impossible. And yet, although he did not fully anticipate the criticisms to come, he was uneasy about what might happen if there were no first principle to stabilize knowledge and guarantee meaning. Consequently, throughout his writings, there sounds a ground bass of concern about the meaningless re-iterations to which we would be condemned if our discourse lacked the foundations he was convinced it required. What I have called Spinoza's bad dream is the accumulating effect of his repeated imagining of an infinite, unanchored series of repetitions, an interminable rootlessness, un-grounded and perpetually unstable. In this way, Spinoza anticipated something of what Durkheim identified as *anomie*, and although Spinoza's bad dream has not explicitly drawn notice, its presence is felt in his writing much as the force of a poem is felt before we come to a fuller understanding of its governing themes and strategies.

In approaching Van Gogh, I have argued that Modernism emerges from the blueprint of Modernity as laid down by Spinoza, and that Van Gogh is an early representative of the Modernist movement. Throughout his life, he wrestled with *anomie*, eventually coming to see his own isolation and rootlessness as part of the agony of the times in which he lived. Art was the main means by which he combatted the worst effects of Spinoza's bad dream, and I have suggested that the path by which he discovered his vocation as a painter recapitulated the cultural narrative itself of the emergence of Modernism from Modernity. As a radically reformed evangelist, a moral reformer who was a scathing critic of traditional religion, an advocate of the healing power of nature and a devotee of the aesthetic who went on to explore the limits of art in order to find a new kind of religious sensibility, Van Gogh repeats within his own career the main cultural crises from which the Modernist movement emerged. This process can best be followed in his letters, on which I have concentrated in the present study. And yet, his correspondence and his paintings work symbiotically, and the cultural recapitulation described in the letters can help us to see the paintings in new ways, as a separate study could profitably confirm. For now, with these points in mind, I have considered also how Van Gogh's changing opinions about drawing show how he moved from a narrative style for representing his moral concerns, to a phase when the drawing was absorbed by a new interest in colour, and then to a further stage in which drawing became a means of exploring how non-realism and self-reflexivity in painting can test the limits of the aesthetic, thereby prising open a space for a renewed sense of the infinite, "something greater than myself", a religion as yet with "no name". As with Spinoza's bad dream, the cultural narrative that I have described as embedded in Van Gogh's correspondence has not previously drawn notice, but it affects readers nonetheless, and the extraordinary interest in Van Gogh's life and work today cannot be separated from the felt impact of his retelling from within his own story the story of all of us who inherit the benefits and challenges of a modern secular society.

My placing of Spinoza and Van Gogh within a narrative about the emergence of Modernism from Modernity is part of a much greater story, the further pursuit of which, as I have pointed out, would lead us back all the way to the untellable beginnings. The self, however provisional and incompletely described, has a narrative structure, and, as with the entire mosaic of our communication skills, we are constituted by a network of stories, none of which is complete but which need not therefore be undependable, often for highly practical purposes. All that we have been remains in what we are, and whatever values our conversations bring to light, if they are worth living by, will reach into the pre-articulate recesses of our embodied selves, engaging us personally and not just conceptually. As Van Gogh well knew, art is a mimesis of this process, and insofar as art invites us to confront the mystery of origins and ends, it is also a prolegomenon to a religious view of the world. In turn, such a view stands opposed to loss of meaning, isolation and rootlessness. In setting out some aspects of how this is so, I have suggested that one main antidote to *anomie* is a recovery of the narratives of its emergence, and therefore also of the countervailing values that such a recovery brings once more to light and which religion might effectively promulgate through a rule of life entailing a further, life-affirming ontological commitment. In offering new perspectives on Spinoza and Van Gogh, I also raise for consideration the fact that the significance of the past is not fixed. Changing historical circumstances can enable the discovery of an unnoticed potential in past events which then gains explanatory power, helping us, amongst other things, to assess future possibilities including a renovated religious understanding, which might, in turn, promote and serve the interests of a common good.

Index

Note: Page numbers followed by "n" denote notes.

For Product Safety Concerns and Information please contact our EU
representative GPSR@taylorandfrancis.com
Taylor & Francis Verlag GmbH, Kaufingerstraße 24, 80331 München, Germany

www.ingramcontent.com/pod-product-compliance
Lightning Source LLC
LaVergne TN
LVHW010936110826
845149LV00013B/2623
* 9 7 8 1 0 3 2 9 0 2 7 2 2 *